WALKING ON THE
ISLE OF MAN

About the Author

Terry has a particular interest in the Isle of Man, having visited the island frequently as a child, and more latterly as a travel journalist. He was the prime mover in 2004 in setting up the island's annual walking festival.

Terry was born into a Lancashire mining family, but escaped the clutches of the National Coal Board to enter local government, wherein he remained until 1990, by which time his first books had been published. A few years as a driving instructor helped to bolster his earnings as a writer, before going full time and trusting to his pen.

He holds a PhD in Historical Geography and an MA in Lake District Studies and is a Fellow of the Royal Geographical Society (FRGS) and of the Society of Antiquaries of Scotland (FSA Scot), as well as a Life Member of the Outdoor Writers and Photographers Guild.

Other Cicerone guides by the author

Geocaching in the UK
Great Mountain Days in Snowdonia
Great Mountain Days in the Pennines
The Coast to Coast Walk
The Dales Way
The Severn Way
The West Highland Way
Walking on the Isle of Mull
Walking on the West Pennine Moors
Walking on the Isle of Skye
Walking in the Forest of Bowland and Pendle

WALKING ON THE ISLE OF MAN

by Terry Marsh

2 POLICE SQUARE, MILNTHORPE, CUMBRIA LA7 7PY
www.cicerone.co.uk

© Terry Marsh 2015
Second edition 2015
ISBN: 978 1 85284 768 5
First edition 2004
ISBN: 978 1 85284 399 1

Printed in China on behalf of Latitude Press Ltd

A catalogue record for this book is available from the British Library.
All photographs are by the author unless otherwise stated.

Dedication

To my wife Vivienne, who walked them all with me, come rain or shine, and in memory of our faithful dog, Teal, who did likewise for the first edition, but sadly was no longer with us when we came to do the second.

Updates to this Guide

While every effort is made by our authors to ensure the accuracy of guidebooks as they go to print, changes can occur during the lifetime of an edition. Any updates that we know of for this guide will be on the Cicerone website (www.cicerone.co.uk/768/updates), so please check before planning your trip. We also advise that you check information about such things as transport, accommodation and shops locally. Even rights of way can be altered over time. We are always grateful for information about any discrepancies between a guidebook and the facts on the ground, sent by email to info@cicerone.co.uk or by post to Cicerone, 2 Police Square, Milnthorpe LA7 7PY, United Kingdom.

Front cover: The cliffs of Spanish Head (Walk 34)

CONTENTS

Acknowledgements

In particular I acknowledge the generous support given to me by the Isle of Man Department of Tourism during the writing of the first edition. I must also place on record my indebtedness to Daphne Caine and Howard Grundey, both of whom kindly read the original manuscript for me, corrected my mistakes and offered many helpful suggestions. Any errors that remain are mine.

Route symbols on OS map extracts
(for OS legend see printed OS maps)

 route

variant/extension/shortcut

 start/finish point

 start point

 finish point

◀ route direction

0 ———————————— 1km

0 ———————————— 0.5 mile

The extracts from 1:50,000 OS maps
used in this book have been reproduced
at 1:40,000 for greater clarity

Features on the overview map

 A road

 ferry route

○ town/village

⊕ airport

600m
400m
200m
75m
0m

Descending into Glen Maye (Walk 22)

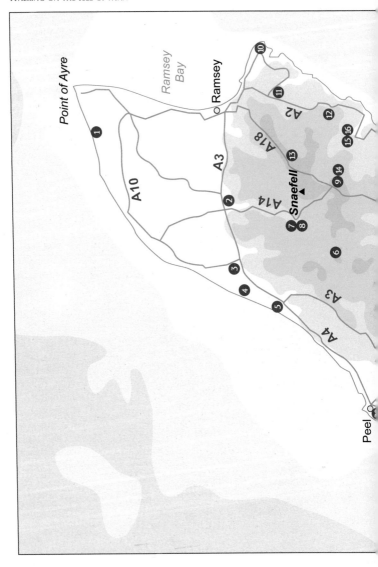

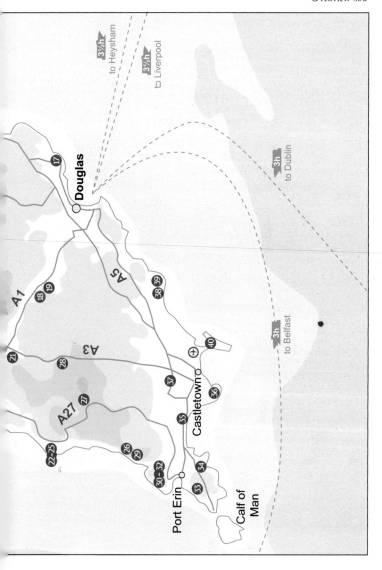

9

Looking forward to Niarbyl from Lhiattee ny Beinnee (Walk 31)

INTRODUCTION

The northern tip of the island seen from the Millennium Way above Ramsay

For most people, the Isle of Man is an enigma: often heard, sadly, is the comment 'I've always wanted to go, but never got round to it'.

Few would think of the island as a walker's paradise – yet it is, as this book will demonstrate. Fewer still know anything about the island, save that it has an annual motorcycle race of some severity, that it is something of a tax haven, that Manx cats have no tails, and (I'm pushing it now) the island's bishop has the title 'Bishop of Sodor and Man'. Very few could explain the way the island is governed: is it part of Britain? (no); the United Kingdom? (no); the Commonwealth,

then? (yes). Yet, the Isle of Man is at the very centre (give or take) of the British Isles, roughly equidistant from the other countries. Indeed, they say that on a clear day it is possible to see seven kingdoms: England, Scotland, Wales, Ireland, Man, and the kingdoms of Heaven and the Sea.

ABOUT THE ISLE OF MAN

The name of the island has some interesting derivations. Julius Caesar mentions an island 'In the middle of the Channel' (by which he meant the Irish Sea), which he called 'Mona', a name also associated with Anglesey,

Above Sulby Reservoir (Walk 7)

off the North Wales coast. This confusion wasn't eased when Pliny the Elder, writing in AD74, listed the islands between Britain and Ireland, and included Mona, by which he probably meant Anglesey, and Monapia, which is thought to have been the Isle of Man. Paulus Orosius (circa AD400) refers to 'Menavia', a place 'of no mean size, with fertile soil, inhabited by a tribe of Scots'. The geographer who visited Britain at the time of Hadrian called the island 'Monaoida', while an Irish monk, Nennius (AD858), refers to 'Eubonia'. Later still, the Irish and Welsh forms become more consistently used, 'Mannan' and 'Mannaw' respectively. The first name-form occurring on the island is on a runic cross in Kirk Michael, 'Maun'. Today, it is known as 'Mannin', 'Vannin' or 'Ellan

Vannin', the island of Man. Those of a more romantic inclination, however, will opt for the view that the name refers to a Celtic sea god, Manannan, the equivalent of the Roman sea god, Neptune, or the Greek, Poseidon.

An island in the Irish Sea, situated mid-way between England, Scotland, Ireland and Wales, the Isle of Man has a land mass of some 572km^2 (221 square miles) and measures, at its extremities, 52km (32½ miles) by 22km (13¾ miles). Geographically it is part of the British Isles, a dependency of the British crown, but it is not part of the United Kingdom. The capital is Douglas, and other towns of size are Ramsey, Peel and Castletown. Government of the island is through the 24 representatives of the House of Keys and a nine-member legislative council, which together make up the

Court of Tynwald (the oldest surviving parliamentary body in continuous existence in the world), passing laws subject to the royal assent. Laws passed at Westminster only affect the island if adopted by Tynwald.

The principal industries are light engineering, agriculture, fishing, tourism, banking and insurance. The island, which has a population of 86,683 (2014), produces its own coins and notes in UK currency denominations, and while UK money can be used on the island, Manx notes are not accepted in the UK. The language is English, though there is a true Manx language, closer to Scottish than Irish Gaelic, which almost died out last century but which has increased in popularity recently. Today, Manx Gaelic is spoken by 2.2 per cent of the total population, a figure which rises to 6.5 per cent in the north of the island.

What the island lacks in size it makes up for in its variety of scenery, which reflects almost every type of landscape found elsewhere in the British Isles, from open moorland to thickly wooded glens, sandy beaches to bare mountain tops, limestone spreads to volcanic basalts. The principal rivers are the Santon, the Silver Burn, the Neb-Thenass, the Sulby and the Dhoo and Glass (ie Douglas). Within the 160km (99 miles) of coastline lies a central range of mountains and hills running north-easterly/south-westerly, from which well-defined valleys descend to cliffs and sheltered bays. In the north of the island the landscape is flat and crossed by slow-moving rivers and streams that debouche onto long sandy beaches. Cutting obliquely across the island, generally at right angles to the main axis, is a central valley with Peel at its western end and Douglas at its eastern.

The watershed, or water-parting, which follows the north-east–south-west axis, has long been important as the fundamental line of separation of the island into 'Northside' and 'Southside' – though this is not the division used in this book, which settles for the much more prosaic division based on the trans-island A1 road. Traditionally, Northside has included the 'sheadings' (districts) of Glenfaba, Michael and Ayre, while Southside embraced Garff, Middle and Rushen sheadings. Changes in 1796 modified the original pattern by making Northside include Michael, Ayre and Garff, and Southside, Glenfaba, Rushen and Middle – a more geographically accurate division.

HISTORY AND CULTURE

The earliest evidence for man's settlement on the island comes from the Mesolithic period, a time when, quite probably, the island still formed part of the British 'mainland'. By Neolithic times (about 6000–4500 years ago), Man was an island, and its people lived around the coastal plains in areas that were covered by predominantly oak woodlands.

Tower, Rushen Abbey

During the Bronze Age (about 4000 years ago), trade in gold ornaments and bronze artefacts extended across Europe, and the Isle of Man clearly played a part in this trade. Towards the end of this period, the climate changed noticeably and for a while the development of the island slowed down, only regaining momentum with the development of Christianity. This was a time when the Romans populated much of Britain, though they never occupied Man, in spite of the probability that they must have passed close to it en route with supplies for the garrison manning Hadrian's Wall, and quite possibly glimpsed it as they trekked to and from their Lakeland fort at Hardknott.

Close contact with Man and the Atlantic coast of Britain continued after the Romans retreated. During this time, between the 5th and 8th centuries, it is probable that the Isle of Man featured in the itineraries of many Christian missionaries. St Bridget, St Ninian, St Patrick, St Columba and St Cuthbert all figure in church dedications on the island, so it is not too fanciful to suppose that they must have arrived here at some time during their lifetimes.

The scene altered significantly with the conquest of the island by Vikings. This brought about many changes in ethnic make-up, religion and cultural identity. Although pagan at the outset, the Norse quickly succumbed to the influence of Christianity. This, in turn, fostered the propagation of a unique blend of Celtic and Norse influences. The most notable survivor from this period is the Norse annual open-air assembly, the 'Thing', at which new laws were announced and disputes settled. In the Norse language, the place for a meeting was a *vollr*, hence *Thing-vollr*, has become Tynwald, the island's unique focus of government.

During this Scandinavian period the Isle of Man became the capital of an island realm – the Kingdom of the Isles – that embraced all the Hebrides, ruled by a Manx king subordinate to Norwegian sovereignty, with its headquarters on St Patrick's Isle, today linked to Peel by a substantial causeway. In a religious context, this became known as Ecclesia Sodorensis, a separate diocese, its name based on the Norse for Man and the Hebrides ('the Southern Isles'). In 1266 the Hebrides were ceded to Scotland, heralding the political break-up of the Kingdom of the Isles, but the religious ties continued for much longer and, though long since severed, there is a reminder of this past regime in the title of the Manx Bishop of Sodor and Man.

For over 100 years, sovereignty of the Isle of Man was disputed between the English and the Scots, with the former ultimately gaining control in 1405 when sovereignty was granted to Sir John Stanley. His descendants – Earls of Derby and Dukes of Atholl – ruled Man for over 300 years, bringing a period of consolidation during which the island became increasingly isolated. This enabled the development of its own form of government, language and personal names. Trade was not encouraged, indeed strictly regulated, and visitors were kept away. The language of the people was Manx – though the well-to-do and government officials spoke English. Castletown was the capital of the island and the place of the lord's residence, finally being displaced in favour of Douglas only in 1869.

During the 17th century, conditions started to change rather radically as 'the running trade' – smuggling – took hold. Man's strategic position, helped by its low custom duties, made it ideal for this form of activity, which grew to such proportions that by the 18th century it became necessary for the British government to 'take control' by introducing the Revesting and Mischief Act in 1765. These effectively meant that sovereignty of the island was once more vested in the Crown, and smuggling was curtailed.

The 'Revestment' was a humiliation and an economic disaster for the Manx people, for although Tynwald still remained, it could pass no laws costing money because the customs duties were diverted to the British government. This situation continued until 1866, when the Manx customs revenue was transferred back to the island's revenue, but with the stipulation that ultimate control over spending should rest with the British Treasury. This situation was only repealed in 1958, since when the island has had the freedom to conduct its own affairs.

GEOLOGY AND VEGETATION

The bulky upland mass of the island is a much-mangled thrust of old slaty rocks, known as the Manx slate series, consisting of clay slates, grits and greywackes, probably Ordovician, rather like the Skiddaw slates of the English Lake District, which also re-appear in the south-west of that region. The slates were refolded several times during the Caledonian mountain-building period and outcrop now in the axis of the island. During this time, the rock mass was penetrated by molten material that formed dykes, most noticeable along the coast, where the slates or grits are exposed.

15

The Bay at Port Cornaa (Walk 11)

During Carboniferous times the limestone that proliferates around Castletown (especially at Scarlett Point) and Port St Mary were laid down. Near Peel, distinctive red sandstone provides an easily work-able material for building stone and appears, along with Castletown limestone, in many buildings on the island.

Solid rocks at surface level are rare, though Carboniferous, Permian and Triassic deposits lie beneath the lowlands at the northern end of the island, covered by glacial drift to a depth of 50m (164ft) or more.

Three successive glacial peri-ods are thought to have affected the island, with glacial deposits most noticeable in the north, but still significant elsewhere. The ice sheets came mainly from south-west Scotland and north-east Ireland, and boulder clays, along with sands and gravels, are distributed over much of the island.

An unusual feature of the Manx landscape, something that has existed for centuries, is the almost complete absence of trees. It is clear that when humans first arrived, the coastal lands would have been covered in oak woods, but today trees only occur in the sheltered glens and in recently re-afforested areas.

A WEALTH OF WILD FLOWERS

The immense diversity of habitat on the Isle of Man generates a range

Cattle at Port Grenaugh

of flora and fauna bordering on the spectacular. There are wild flowers throughout the year, from the primroses, celandine, sorrel and wood anemones of spring, when rafts of wild garlic are already filling the air with their pungent smell and bluebells (blue, white and pink in hue) are starting to carpet whatever remaining stands of woodland they can find. Gorse is already in heady, scented bloom come early April, when the delicate coastal squill, sea campion and thrift are also starting to flower. Orchids flourish in June, while the heathers that bring a purple hue to the Manx hillsides start to flower from July onwards.

Later in the year, into autumn, a few sheltered woodland spots start to produce fungi as the great colour change of the year begins. Throughout the year it is impossible not to notice the luxuriant growth of lichens, mosses and liverworts – clear indicators of a clean and healthy climate.

BIRDLIFE

The island is well suited to birdlife, and a free leaflet from tourist information centres tells you where to look, and when, for the island's most interesting species.

You may be able to spot red-throated, black-throated and great northern divers, Manx shearwater, storm petrel, water rail, hen harrier, bar-tailed godwit, long- and short-eared owls, siskin, redpoll, crossbill and chough. See Appendix C for information about the work of the Manx Wildlife Trust.

CLIMATE

Because of the influence of the Irish Sea, the Manx climate is temperate and lacking in extremes. In winter, snowfall and frost are infrequent. On rare occasions snow does occur, but seldom lies for more than a day or two. February tends to be the coldest month, with an average daily temperature of 4.9°C (41°F), but it is also often dry. However, the island is rather windy. The prevailing wind direction for most of the island is from the south-west, although the complex topography means that local effects of shelter and exposure are very variable. April, May and June are the driest months, while May, June and July are the sunniest. July and August are the warmest months, with an average daily maximum temperature around 17.6°C (63°F). The highest temperature recorded at the island's weather centre at Ronaldsway is 28.9°C, or 84°F. Thunderstorms are infrequent and short-lived.

Although geographically small, there is, nevertheless, significant climatic variation around the island. Sea fog affects the southern and eastern coasts at times, especially in spring, but is less frequent in the west. Rainfall and the frequency of hill fog both increase with altitude. The highest point of the island – Snaefell at 621m (2036ft) – receives some 2¼ times more rainfall than Ronaldsway, on the south-east coast, where the annual average is 863mm (34ins).

Niarbyl (Walk 23)

St Michael's Island (Walk 40)

THE THREE LEGS OF MAN

No one really knows how the Three Legs of Man motif, the symbol of independence, came to be adopted as the national emblem of the Isle of Man. The three-legged device certainly has a long history, dating far back into pagan times, and represents the sun and its daily passage across the heavens. The Manx form was derived from a design that showed the spokes of a wheel and which, in turn, represented the rays of the sun. This has led to it being described as a solar wheel, a symbol of pagan sun worship. Other related symbols include the cross and the fylfot, or four-legged swastika.

It is believed that Alexander III of Scotland may have adopted it when he gained control of the Isle of Man following the defeat of King Haakon of Norway at Largs in 1263 and the end of Norse rule that followed. Credence is given to this notion by the fact that the seal of King Harald Olaffson, granting a mining charter to the monks of Furness Abbey in 1246, still bore a ship emblem as its seal, not the Three Legs motif. The oldest representation of the Three Legs in existence is on the Manx Sword of State, and there is another use on the Maughold Market Cross, now in St Maughold's Church.

GETTING THERE

It might be worth checking the sporting calendar before beginning to plan your trip, as the famous TT (Tourist Trophy) motorbike race and the Grand Prix rather take over the island when they're on, and there are other races throughout the year. The main TT weeks are late May/early June and the Grand Prix is late August/early September.

By air

Frequent flights are provided to and from London (Gatwick, Heathrow and Southend), Manchester, Liverpool, Bristol, Blackpool, Birmingham, Glasgow, Gloucester, Leeds/Bradford, Jersey and Dublin. There are also connecting flights linking the island to Newcastle, Edinburgh, East Midlands and Southampton and to many international destinations.

On arrival on the island, you are greeted with a very modern airport terminal, with an assortment of shops, café, seating areas and telephones. Security checks exist, as in all UK national airports. In addition, flights to and from Ireland are subject to duty free allowances.

Getting through the airport is relatively quick compared to UK airports. Immediately outside the airport terminal is the main bus route and stop for travelling to Douglas and the south. Inside the terminal are a number of car hire firms.

By sea

The island's principal port is Douglas, which has deep-water berths and facilities for handling passengers, cars and freight vehicles and general cargoes. Peel, on the west coast, has a deep-water berth and facilities for handling limited passenger traffic and general cargoes. Ramsey in the northeast is a drying harbour with a busy trade in general and bulk cargoes.

The island's main sea routes are between Douglas and Liverpool, and Douglas and Heysham, a modern port in the north-west of England closely linked to Britain's motorway and intercity rail networks. The Isle of Man Steam Packet Company operates multi-purpose and freight RORO vessels on the Heysham route, providing twice-daily services throughout the year for passengers, cars and freight vehicles. The Steam Packet Company also has twice-daily fast craft services from Liverpool from April to October and conventional weekend services during the winter.

In the summer months the Steam Packet operates additional fast craft routes for holiday traffic to Dublin and Belfast, as well as extra sailings to Heysham and Liverpool with SeaCat and SuperSeaCat fast craft.

GETTING ABOUT

By car or motor bike

Driving around the island is generally relaxed and enjoyable. Typical A- and B-roads, together with country lanes, prevail. Speed limits vary across the island, and the best advice is to stay below 30mph in built-up areas and 50mph elsewhere.

Many of the roads and lanes are narrow and twisting, and must be negotiated with care. It is an offence, as it is in the UK, to use a hand-held mobile phone while driving. Seatbelt laws apply on the island as they do throughout the UK. All vehicles must be insured and you should have your driving licence with you. Although not mandatory, it's advisable to have vehicle breakdown cover, and a first aid kit, warning triangle and fire extinguisher.

Parking discs, available free from a number of locations, including the Sea Terminal Building, are required in the larger towns and villages. Disc parking zones, which are clearly signed, range from 15 minutes to two hours. Trailer caravans are not permitted on the island, but tenting campers and self-propelled motor caravans are welcome.

Because of the wide range of events held on the island each year, there are times when many of the roads will be closed for short periods. Information about road closures and events can be obtained from the Welcome Centre at the Sea Terminal Building.

Steam train
Running in the summer season (Easter to September) from Douglas to Port Erin, the steam train takes about 1 hour for the journey, with several stations to stop off on the way. Tickets are available from the main stations. Douglas Station is about 10 minutes' walk from the Sea Terminal.

Horse-drawn tram
The horse-drawn trams complete a circuit along Douglas promenade, from outside the Sea Terminal to Derby Castle at the opposite end of the promenade. These operate during the summer season only. Travel time is approximately 30 minutes each way. Tickets can be purchased on board.

Electric train
The Manx Electric Railway operates all year round, except Christmas week, from Douglas promenade (Derby Castle) all the way to Laxey. You then have a choice to continue to Ramsey or (summer only) take the alternative route up Snaefell on the Snaefell Mountain Railway branch line.

The time to Laxey is about 30 minutes. From there to Ramsey is about the same, and the trip to the summit of Snaefell takes about 40 minutes.

Bus
A national bus service operates throughout the island, connecting all the towns, villages and district areas. The frequency of the different services depends very much on the nature of the destination and the departure points. Prices are relatively cheap and multi-day passes can be purchased. Isle of Man resident OAPs travel for free – but there are no concessions for visiting pensioners.

Taxi
There are taxi ranks in all the main urban centres.

Car hire

Hire cars are available at the Sea Terminal, the airport terminal, delivered to your hotel or picked up at certain garages. Booking is advised. You will need to be 21 or over, have a valid driving licence and possibly your passport.

ACCOMMODATION

There is a wide range of excellent accommodation, from prime hotels to inexpensive B&Bs and self-catering properties right across the island, though there are no hostels as such, and few campsites. All the walks in this book were completed from bases at Orrisdale (Kirk Michael) and Colby Glen (First edition), and Crosby (Second edition), but the island's road and public transport network is such that it matters not which town or village is used.

WALKING AND ACCESS

The scope for walking on the island is considerable, and with a very distinctive flavour. Being an island, and a smallish one at that, many walks touch upon the coastline at some point, and it is almost true to say that on every walk in this book you can see the sea at some stage. It is equally valid that with few exceptions all the footpaths are well signed, whether it is for the normal paths or one (or more) of the long- and middle-distance trails that criss-cross the island.

There is limited opportunity for walks in excess of, say, 16km (10

Looking across the bay to Bradda Hill (Walk 30)

miles), though the diligent person can string together quite a few smaller walks to make something more demanding. So, the emphasis here is on shorter walks, suitable for half days, or for families. More committed walkers will still find they can spend long days crossing the hills that form the central spine of the island, but the number of opportunities to do so is limited. Even so, you can come here for a month and still follow a new walk every day.

And being so close to the sea produces its own brand of weather conditions for the walker to contend with – from hot balmy days to real howlers on the tops. Sea mist can be quite a problem, too, so if you can't navigate in poor visibility, it would be a good idea to wait for a clear day.

As in the UK great swathes of the Isle of Man are open access, here known as 'Public Ramblage'. In essence this means there is a freedom to roam at will. Large parts of the high ground fall within this definition. Other areas hold 'Scenic Significance' or are held by the Manx National Trust or Manx National Heritage, and here access is generally not a problem, though there may be local restrictions.

Elsewhere, the island has 17 National Glens, maintained and preserved by the Forestry Department, because it is largely in the glens that the island's main areas of tree cover are to be found. There are two types of glen, coastal and mountain. The coastal glens – like Glen Maye, Groudle Glen, Glen Wyllin and Dhoon Glen – often lead down to a beach, while the mountain glens – Sulby, Glen Mooar, Colby Glen – have splendid streams, waterfalls and pools.

Spread across the island is a network of 'Greenway Roads' and 'Green Lanes'. A Green Lane is an unsurfaced road through the countryside for pedestrians, 4x4s, motorcycles, mountain bikes and horses, similar to a Byway Open to All Traffic in England. Some are 'Greenway Roads' which have restrictions. On Green Lanes, vehicle users should give way to pedestrians and horse riders, and be aware that farm animals may be in the road at any time.

MAPPING

One of the problems, probably the only significant problem, for walkers visiting the island is the mapping. The British Ordnance Survey produces a single Landranger map (Sheet 95), at a scale of 1:50,000, and experienced walkers will find this adequate. But, at the time of writing the first edition, there was no corresponding larger scale OS map. What existed was a two-sheet 1:25,000 Outdoor Leisure Map produced by the Isle of Man by reducing old six-inch maps. The result was often text too small to read with the naked eye, although rights of way were clearly depicted. This has been replaced by a more modern map which is a little better in this respect.

Walking across Maughold Brooghs (Walk 10)

A modern 1:30,000 map, produced by Harvey Maps, is probably the best map for walkers.

USING THIS GUIDE

The walks range across the whole island and are grouped, roughly equally, North or South, on no stronger relationship than that they have with the A1 Douglas to Peel road. There is no other geographical significance to the grouping.

The descriptions in this guidebook all follow the same format. The information box gives the stage start and finish location accompanied by grid references, stage distance (km/miles), height gain, details of places close to the route that offer refreshments and hints on parking.

The map extracts which accompany each route are taken from the 1:50,000 OS mapping, blown up to 1:40,000 for greater clarity. A summary table of all walks in the guidebook, to help you select the most convenient route for you and your walking party, can be found in Appendix A.

THE NORTH

Track leading through Glen Mona (Walk 11)

WALK 1

Ayres, Point of Ayre and Bride

Start/Finish	Ayres Visitor Centre (NX 435 038)
Distance	12km (7½ miles)
Height gain	80m (262ft)
Refreshments	Tea room in Bride
Parking	At visitor centre

This walk is for birdwatchers and those who love being close to the sea. The island's northern coastline plays host to almost every species of bird listed for the island at some time during each year, and invariably includes many interesting migratory, passage birds. Unfortunately there is quite a bit of road walking to make the walk into a proper circuit, and this detracts from the walk a little as well as introducing a note of danger as the roads are not pedestrian-friendly, having neither footpaths nor verges. Consider retracing your steps from Phurt rather than risking the road section, especially if there are young, elderly or animals in the party, although Bride is always worth a visit.

AYRES NATIONAL NATURE RESERVE

The nature reserve has a total area of 272ha (673 acres). The site is internationally important for breeding birds, and the whole area of outstanding interest for natural historians. Out at sea gannet, shag, cormorant, guillemot, and little, common and arctic terns are frequent visitors – along with the occasional black-throated and great northern diver. Don't be surprised to spot the dorsal fins of whales and porpoises, as well as the bobbing heads of grey seals. Along the shore, and inland among the dunes and heath, expect to find ringed plover, oystercatcher, sanderling, dunlin, curlew, stonechat, skylark and whinchat. Wild flowers are especially rich here, and include pyramidal and early purple orchids, wild thyme and burnet rose. From 1 April to 31 July, dogs must be on a lead.

Fishermen favour this northernmost tip of the island, and can often be seen here, shore casting for mackerel or plaice.

From the **Ayres National Nature Reserve Visitor Centre** (rarely open as it is staffed by volunteers), either take to a grassy track starting from near the information panels heading towards the distant lighthouse, or walk back along the access road for about 50m to a paved path that sets you off in the same direction, but with firmer footing, something that will be appreciated at certain times of the year. When the paving ends, the path joins the grassy track, running close enough to the upper level of the beach to give good sightings of the birdlife here.

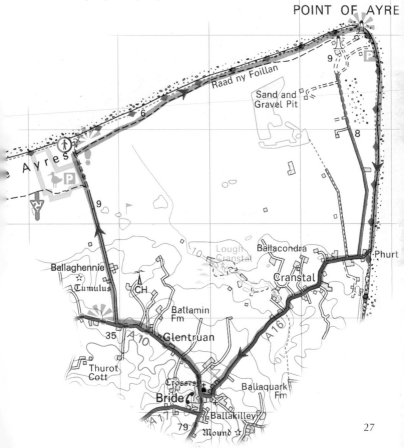

Ayres National Nature Reserve is a favoured breeding ground for birds, so during the breeding season care needs to be exercised in the placement of one's feet, and any dogs need the control of a tight rein.

Regular visitors to the reserve include ringed plover, little tern, common/Arctic tern, oystercatcher, curlew, black-throated diver, eider, shag, cormorant, gannet, stonechat, meadow pipit and skylark.

The grassy track leads on steadily to the **Point of Ayre lighthouse**.

The Point of Ayre **lighthouse** – controlled by the Northern Lights Board of Scotland, not Trinity House, as might be supposed – was built between 1815 and 1818 by Robert Stevenson, the grandfather of Robert Louis Stevenson.

The Point of Ayre lighthouse

Just beyond the lighthouse, the coastline heads south, so either bear right or get your feet wet. Offshore, it is not

unusual to be treated to the sight of some turbulent water: two different tidal systems meet here and produce quite a frenzy on a good day. But on dry land, the route heads south, and continues just above the shore edge as far as a couple of cottages at Phurt. It is possible to turn inland a little earlier than this, when the ongoing track does so, but otherwise a narrow, field-edge path leads on to **Phurt**.

From here on, all is road walking; first to the lovely village of **Bride**, with its church dedicated to St Bridget. And from there along the A10, through **Glentruan**, continuing as far as the turning to **Ballaghennie Farm** (NX 439 019). There, turn right, down a road lovely in spring with wild flowers, leading back to the shore at the visitor centre.

WALK 2
Sulby and the Millennium Way

Start/Finish	Sulby Claddagh (SC 386 940)
Distance	10km (6¼ miles)
Height gain	358m (1175ft)
Parking	Small car park by the river

This is an exhilarating walk, beginning beside the Sulby River and climbing high onto the gorse uplands to the south. Choose a clear day (the map, the signposting and the paths don't always agree and in poor visibility this could be a problem), and enjoy the airy freedom of mountain heath patrolled by hen harriers, kestrels and short-eared owls.

Set off alongside the Sulby River, going with the flow and parallel with a road, and when this bends right, go with it, soon to reach a bridge spanning an in-flowing burn. Ignore the bridge, and keep forward on a gently rising lane (signposted 'Snaefell Mountain Road'). Walk up the lane until the road surfacing ends and there branch left over a stile beside a gate, giving onto a rough track rising steadily to the edge of **Ohio Plantation**.

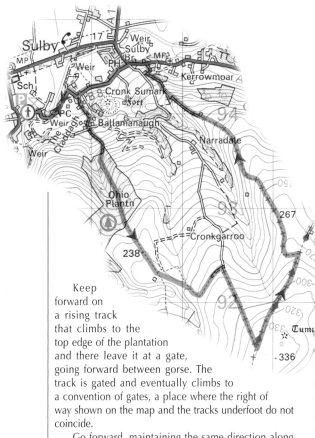

Keep
forward on
a rising track
that climbs to the
top edge of the plantation
and there leave it at a gate,
going forward between gorse. The
track is gated and eventually climbs to
a convention of gates, a place where the right of
way shown on the map and the tracks underfoot do not
coincide.

Go forward, maintaining the same direction along
a broad track with an earth embankment on the right.
Continue up the track until a signpost directs the route
left to a larger-than-normal ladder/stile. Over this, turn
left again, along a broad grassy track, and keep going to
a gate in a fence corner. From there, go forward through
heather on a rough track that closes in on a wall on the
left as it approaches two metal gates at the top of a rough
road descending left to Sulby.

From the gates (ignore the road), turn right and strike up the heather moorland on a rutted track for just under 1km (½ mile). Keep going until the gradient levels as the track starts to swing towards the masted summit of Snaefell, and then look for a short branching track on the left, cutting through low heather to intercept the Millennium Way (though there is nothing immediate to confirm that it is the Millennium Way). Turn left, soon passing a right of way sign. ▶

Now gently descending, with a fine view northwards across Sulby to the conspicuous white church at Jurby and the Ayres Nature Reserve, go as far as another gate at the head of a walled track. Here, without going through the gate, turn left alongside a wall to another gate giving onto a sunken track.

This track now leads all the way back to Sulby. Part way down it becomes partially surfaced, and is flanked throughout by gorse, stitchwort, violet, celandine, wild garlic, bluebell and intermittent stands of holly.

The track eventually descends to meet the main Sulby to Ramsey road. Take care emerging onto the road. Turn left and shortly go left again at the Ginger Hall Hotel.

Striding out along the Millennium Way above Sulby

Later, a low sign does indeed confirm that you are on the Millennium Way.

Turn left into River Meadow Lane, following this back lane past the prehistoric site of Cronkshamerk (**Cronk Sumark**) hill fort (accessible by a steep climb from the roadside), after which you reach the road bridge encountered at the start of the walk. Cross it and turn right to follow the road back to the starting point.

WALK 3

Slieu Curn and Slieu Dhoo

Start/Finish	Ballaugh (SC 348 935)
Distance	17.3km (10¾ miles)
Height gain	445m (1460ft)
Refreshments	Ballaugh and Sulby
Parking	On-street parking (with care) in Ballaugh

In spite of its length, this walk is fairly straightforward and undemanding, but does offer the option of including Slieu Freoaghane. There is also the possibility of visiting Killabrega, a deserted and ruinous farmstead high up on the western flank of Sulby Glen, although this will entail a longish amount of road walking to complete the route.

In Ballaugh, go down the road past a mini supermarket to a gated turning on the left onto the old railway line. Continue along the trackbed to the first main junction, at a gate, and here turn left and walk out to the main road.

At the road, turn left but after about 100m take the first turning on the right at Ballacob onto a side lane flanked by mature hedgerows. Follow the ascending lane and, when it forks, branch to the right. When the lane turns into **Ballacurnkeil** at the start of a greenway, the Bayr Glass, keep forward onto a dirt track between gorse hedgerows.

Follow the track, rising steadily onto the northern slopes of **Slieu Curn**. As the gradient eases, with Snaefell coming into view and, off to the right, the Mountains of Mourne in Northern Ireland and the hills of Galloway in

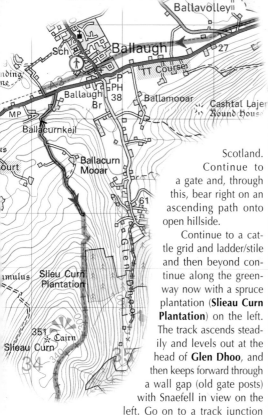

map continues on
page 34

Scotland.
Continue to
a gate and, through
this, bear right on an
ascending path onto
open hillside.
Continue to a cat-
tle grid and ladder/stile
and then beyond con-
tinue along the green-
way now with a spruce
plantation (**Slieau Curn
Plantation**) on the left.
The track ascends stead-
ily and levels out at the
head of **Glen Dhoo**, and
then keeps forward through
a wall gap (old gate posts)
with Snaefell in view on the
left. Go on to a track junction
where the track starts to climb again to meet a rough,
stony track near a signpost. Here, turn onto the stony track,
ignoring a branching green track on the left. Continue up
the stony track, which gradually levels and then descends
a little and runs on to a point below **Slieau Freoaghane**.

Extension to Slieau Freoaghane
Anyone wanting to bag Slieau Freoaghane (one of five
Marilyns on the island) should simply leave the track
here and climb steeply to the summit on a clear, if boggy,
path. The top is adorned by a large pole, trig pillar and
quartz cairn. This will add about 1km (½ mile) to the

Looking back to Slieu Curn from the slopes of Slieau Freoaghane

distance, plus 100m (328ft) of ascent. Come back the same way to rejoin the broad stony track, heading south to Sartfell Plantation.

About 200m after the junction, between the main track and the extension to Slieau Freoaghane, another clear, rutted track branches left, parallel with a wall and alongside a fence. Turn sharply onto this, still waymarked as a greenway, and follow it across the flanks of **Slieau Dhoo**.

The track eventually runs down to meet a gate, where the greenway ends. Keep forward with the ongoing track, which descends to meet a surfaced mountain road. Turn left. As the road later starts to bend to the left, leave it by branching right onto a stony track, once more the Bayr Glass.

Again there is a choice. The main route keeps forward across the western flank of **Mount Karrin** and eventually descends through **Ballacuberagh Plantation** to meet the Sulby Glen road.

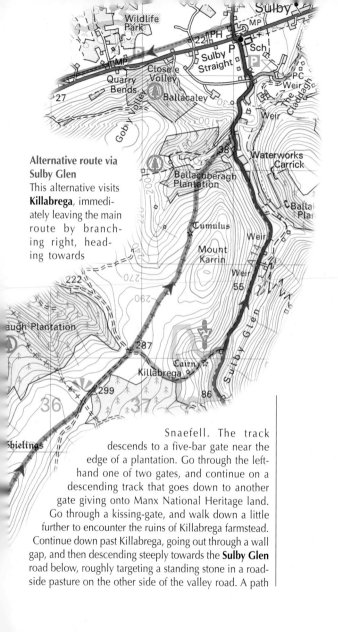

Alternative route via Sulby Glen

This alternative visits **Killabrega**, immediately leaving the main route by branching right, heading towards

Snaefell. The track descends to a five-bar gate near the edge of a plantation. Go through the left-hand one of two gates, and continue on a descending track that goes down to another gate giving onto Manx National Heritage land. Go through a kissing-gate, and walk down a little further to encounter the ruins of Killabrega farmstead. Continue down past Killabrega, going out through a wall gap, and then descending steeply towards the **Sulby Glen** road below, roughly targeting a standing stone in a roadside pasture on the other side of the valley road. A path leads down through an expanse of bracken (seasonally overgrown) and reaches a fence corner where there is a small step/stile. Over this, continue along a steep, zig-zagging path down to the rear of a cottage. Here, bear right along an indistinct path that shortly turns down to reach the Sulby Glen road.

On reaching the road, turn left and, taking care against approaching traffic, follow the valley road all the way to Sulby, passing the main line of the walk below **Ballacuberagh Plantation**.

In Sulby, the continuation heads down the Jurby road, to the right of the Sulby Glen Hotel, until the old railway trackbed is once again encountered. Turn left onto this and keep on, passing the Curraghs **Wildlife Park**, to return to Ballaugh.

WALK 4
Orrisdale and Glen Trunk

Start/Finish	Orrisdale (SC 327 929)
Distance	4.4km (2¾ miles)
Height gain	55m (180ft)
Parking	Limited roadside parking at Orrisdale

This deceptively simple walk is full of interest and has the advantage of seclusion. It wanders quiet lanes, visits the beach and comes back past one of the great seats of power on the island in times gone by.

The first part of the walk heads down the lane through the scattered hamlet of Orrisdale. Just before the Methodist chapel, a lane branches right at an interesting house with a weather vane and pump. This lane leads to a spot marked on the map as a **Cairn**.

Also known as the **Druid's Circle**, on Cronk Koir, this is a pre-Christian site comprising large quartz boulders set in a circle.

Back on the village lane, go past the chapel and follow the lane through a few twists and turns as far as a signed footpath (SC 322 926) branching on the right to

Gorse-lined path through Glen Trunk

37

the seashore. Beyond a gate a delightful grassy path leads down between gorse bushes towards the shore. This is Glen Trunk, quiet, secluded and little visited. The path leads past a lime kiln finally to reach a shoulder overlooking the beach just south of Orrisdale Head.

Just before reaching the seashore, there is a fine **lime kiln** tucked neatly into the flank of Glen Trunk. It is one of the largest and most complete to be found on the island. Although not certain, it is likely that the lime would have been brought into the glen by boat and left on the shore for collection and processing.

Here, dip left to cross a wooden footbridge spanning Glen Trunk burn, climbing on the other side to join a vehicle access lane near an isolated cottage. Follow the lane out to meet a surfaced road. Go briefly left and then through a kissing-gate into a field, following a field edge grassy path to a gate at the top of a narrow track, then head downhill to the trackbed of the railway line that once operated along this stretch of coast.

Turn left onto a footpath following the old trackbed, passing behind the impressive building, **Bishop's Court**.

BISHOP'S COURT

One of the great houses of interest on the island, Bishop's Court's origins are traditionally attributed to Bishop Simon in the 13th century. It was a fortress tower and, in its early days, was moated – the old name for this and the surrounding area was Ballachurrey, which means 'marshy place'. The first mention of the building occurs in 1231, so there was evidently some significant building on this site before Bishop Simon arrived. In those days, the bishop was a vastly powerful man and, in his own right, a baron, with the power of life and death over his subjects, which gave this outpost something akin to the forts that developed throughout the Border Marches of Wales.

Bishop's Court was sold into private hands in 1979, so ending more than seven centuries of association with the Diocese of Sodor and Man.

Bishop's Court

Go onward until the path finally emerges at a lane. Turn left, towards **Orrisdale**, to complete the walk.

WALK 5

Kirk Michael and Slieau Freoaghane

Start/Finish	Kirk Michael (SC 319 909)
Distance	14.5km (9 miles)
Height gain	533m (1750ft)
Refreshments	Kirk Michael
Parking	Kirk Michael

Slieau Freoaghane – which Manx Gaelic speakers advise me is pronounced 'Sloo Ferrane' – is one of five Marilyns on the island, and likely to be popular on that count alone. But it is a fine hill to climb regardless of this dubious distinction, though the shortest, most direct route – and least interesting – is from the cross-mountain road near Sartfell Plantation.

This route partially reverses Walk 3, as far as Ballaugh, but then makes use of the old railway trackbed to return to Kirk Michael. It is a splendid walk, best reserved for a clear day, when the views over the western side of the island and across the Irish Sea to the mountains of Northern Ireland and northwards to southern Scotland are outstanding. There are times when the Mountains of Mourne seem so close you feel you could simply reach out and touch them.

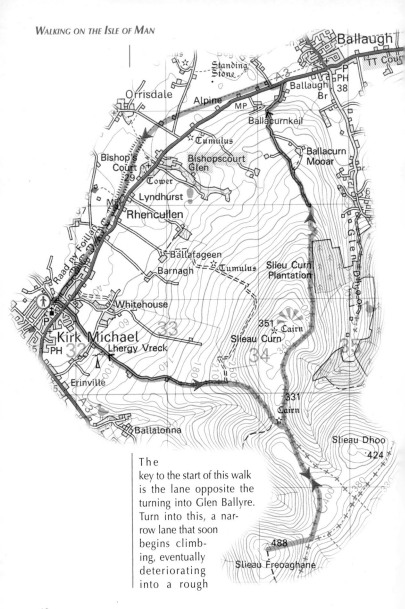

The key to the start of this walk is the lane opposite the turning into Glen Ballyre. Turn into this, a narrow lane that soon begins climbing, eventually deteriorating into a rough

Slieau Freoghane and Slieu Curn from the mountain road

track striking up onto open moorland. High up on the hillside, to the north of Slieau Freoaghane, the track meets a huge **cairn**, Cairn Vael. ▶

Just past the cairn the return track to Ballaugh departs left, and anyone wanting to omit Slieau Freoaghane should turn off here. Otherwise, bear right and continue along the stony track, ignoring a branching green track on the left. Gradually the track levels and then descends a little as it runs on to a point below **Slieau Freoaghane**.

Now simply turn right and climb steeply to the top of Slieau Freoaghane on a clear, if boggy, path. The top is adorned by a trig pillar and quartz cairn.

Retrace the ascent, back to the track junction near Cairn Vael, now keeping forward on a clear track heading for **Slieau Curn** and passing deeply defined Glen Dhoo and **Slieau Curn Plantation** on the right. The onward route is clear and not in doubt, leading eventually to an enclosed grassy track and then a surfaced lane (at **Ballacurnkeil**). Keep on, now following the surfaced lane, which leads down to the Kirk Michael to Ramsey road, not far from **Ballaugh**.

The cairn is largely the product of passing miners in years gone by, who would add another rock every time they walked by as a kind of talisman.

41

Turn left for about 100m and take the first track on the right, which soon intercepts the course of the old railway. Turn left onto this and simply follow it easily for a little over 3.5km (2 miles), passing **Bishop's Court** (see box in Walk 4), back to Kirk Michael.

WALK 6
Slieau Freoaghane and Sartfell

Start/Finish	Sartfell Plantation (SC 342 866)
Distance	5.3km (3½ miles)
Height gain	215m (705ft)
Parking	Parking area near start

This is a simple and direct way of 'bagging' Slieau Freoaghane and the nearby Sartfell. The views are good, but other than that this ascent has little to commend it other than directness – it's a peak bagger's route rather than a hill walker's.

From the Sartfell road go through the gate (signpost) at the south-western corner of **Sartfell Plantation** onto a

Snaefell and Sulby Reservoir from the top of Slieau Freoghane

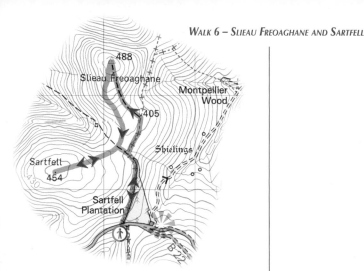

broad track that climbs at first alongside the plantation boundary. ▶

Shortly, having left the plantation behind, the track bends around a stream as it passes onto the broad southern shoulder of **Slieau Freoaghane**. At this point it is possible to bear left and walk easily up through the rough, heathery top of the hill on a variable path.

From the summit retreat on more or less the same line towards the broad grass and heather col with Sartfell, moving more to a south-westerly direction as the col is approached. Then strike up easy slopes onto **Sartfell**, a rounded lump. From the top of the hill any line eastwards will lead down to intercept the upward route from the Sartfell road, but it is easier going to return to the col and pick up the outward route there.

The small plantation – about 10 hectares – was planted in 1964 with Sitka spruce and Lodgepole pine.

WALK 7
Sulby Reservoir

Start/Finish	Sulby Reservoir car park (SC 374 890)
Distance	4.25km (2½ miles)
Height gain	257m (843ft)
Refreshments	Seasonal tea room in Sulby Glen
Parking	At start

This walk is perfect for a warm summer's afternoon, before or after a picnic (there are tables near the start). It is nowhere demanding, and climbs onto the edge of open moorland along a high mountain road with refreshing views across the hinterland of Druidale, before descending along the edge of a sizeable pine plantation.

From the parking area, go down steps and cross the reservoir dam. On the other side, bear right briefly to a gate. Just beyond this, turn left onto a rising track that higher up continues as an agreeable grassy path alongside a fence, and with splendid views of Snaefell and Beinn-y-Phott.

The path eventually drops to a gate and bridge spanning a stream. Climb out on the other side, and go forward through a metal kissing-gate and two farm gates onto an enclosed path that leads up to another kissing-gate near the entrance to **Druidale Farm**. Turn right and follow the farm access out to a narrow mountain road (SC 361 888). Now turn right and

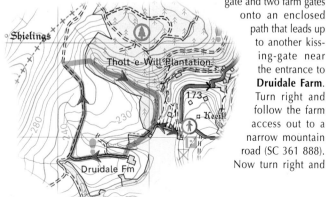

follow the road, passing a lime kiln on the left, and continuing to a gated stony track on the right (SC 362 895) at a road bend.

    Go down the track to a gate and stile giving into the top end of a descending forest trail. Walk easily down this, and, at the bottom, swing right, climbing a little to the gate encountered in the early stages of the walk. Now simply retrace the outward route across the reservoir dam.

Looking down on Sulby Glen and reservoir

45

WALK 8
Upper Sulby Glen

Start/Finish	Sulby Reservoir car park (SC 374 890)
Distance	12km (7½ miles)
Height gain	443m (1453ft)
Refreshments	Seasonal tea room in Sulby Glen
Parking	At start

Sulby Glen is a particular treat, a rather secluded enclave perfect for walkers. Walk 7 gives a short walk near to the reservoir, but here the route goes farther and higher, making the most of a splendid Greenway Road high above the glen.

From the car park, go down steps to the dam of the reservoir. On the other side swing right to a gate and follow a broad path to arrive at the edge of the **Tholt-e-Will Plantation** at a broad forest trail. Here, turn left, and climb gently to a top gate beyond which a track leads out to a narrow mountain road (SC 362 895).

Turn right and follow this, ascending steadily, for about 1km (½ mile), as far as a broad track (a Greenway Road) on the left (SC 363 904). Double back along this to a gate and then continue across the flank of **Slieau Dhoo** to meet a broad stony track just below **Slieau Freoaghane**. Turn left again and follow this track southwards around Slieau Freoaghane and the adjacent Sartfell to meet a road at the edge of **Sartfell Plantation**. ◄

Turn left, ignore the branching road on the right, and continue to the far side of the plantation, where a road branches left – the other end of the same road used earlier. Go along this as far as the turning to **Druidale Farm** (SC 361 888). Leave the road here by walking down the farm access track.

Just before the farm, go left at a signpost, through a metal kissing-gate and down an enclosed path via two farm

On a clear day it is an easy matter to include both Slieau Freoaghane and Sartfell in this walk, by easy and obvious diversions. That onto Slieau Freoaghane is the steeper of the two.

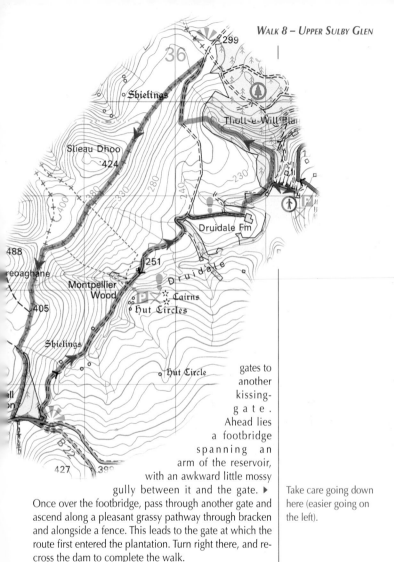

gates to another kissing-gate. Ahead lies a footbridge spanning an arm of the reservoir, with an awkward little mossy gully between it and the gate. ▶

Take care going down here (easier going on the left).

Once over the footbridge, pass through another gate and ascend along a pleasant grassy pathway through bracken and alongside a fence. This leads to the gate at which the route first entered the plantation. Turn right there, and re-cross the dam to complete the walk.

47

WALK 9

A taste of the Millennium Way

Start	Bungalow (SC 396 868)
Finish	Turning into Glen Auldyn (SC 436 944)
Distance	11km (7 miles)
Height gain	210m (690ft)
Transport	You'll need to organise transport to either end, or use public transport

This splendid walk is an unashamed excuse to wander along the Millennium Way and explore some of the wildest landscapes on the island, concluding with a visit to one of the most significant historic sites on the island – Sky Hill. This is not a walk for misty days, when route-finding might be a problem in the early stages, but on a clear day there is an invigorating sensation about the austere moors, where mountain hares dart about and moorland birds erupt dramatically ahead of you. The walk is linear, and walkers will therefore need to arrange transport to and from either end. It is possible, however, to use the Snaefell Mountain Railway from Laxey to reach the Bungalow, and to return by public transport to Ramsey and then by Manx Electric Railway (or buses) either to the start in Laxey or back to Douglas.

The Millennium Way is waymarked throughout, but in places the waymarks are well spaced out, making some of the sections potentially confusing to follow. For some, this will add to the pleasure of the walk, especially as it moves further away from Snaefell. Walkers who are happy wandering across trackless moorland could follow Walk 14 to the summit of Snaefell and then continue onward into the moorland hollow beyond, where you can intercept the Millennium Way and continue with this walk.

The route begins from the Bungalow, where the Snaefell Mountain Railway crosses the mountain road. Here, head down the side road towards Sulby, taking care against approaching traffic, and follow this for 1.8km (just over a mile) until you meet the crossing point of the Millennium Way, at a clear, signed track on the right. Leave the road here, and pick up the waymarked route, which curves easily around Snaefell, becoming less and less distinct as it targets the head of the shallow valley in which **Block Eary** reservoir reposes.

map continues on page 50

> **Sheep** still abound on the moors here, and this was once a favoured place with Manx shepherds, who came here to pasture sheep during the summer months. The scattered hummocks are all that remain of their shielings (s u m m e r homes).

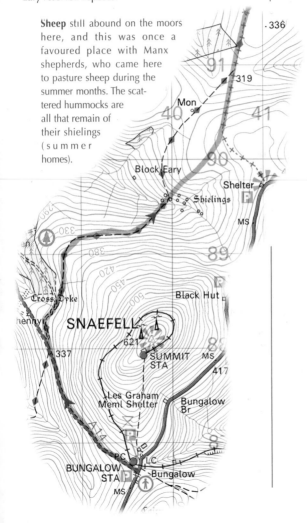

On the watershed is a large and ornate cairn, a conspicuous marker.

Cross a stream and continue on a clear path across the shoulder of **Slieau Managh**, an occasionally marshy affair. ◄

The route leads on to meet a track coming in from the right, from the Mountain Box on the TT course. Stay with the Millennium Way at this junction, which is now followed all the way to the end of the walk.

The track continues to a metal gate in a wall. Beyond this it continues as a rough, stony track across heather moorland, and for a short stretch shares part of the Way with Walk 2. A wide sweep of moorland, patrolled by hen harriers, ravens and snipe, leads eventually to another metal gate and signpost ('Sky Hill 3m').

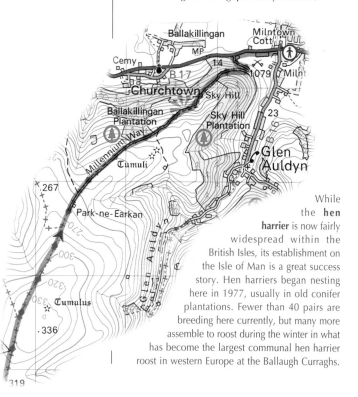

While the **hen harrier** is now fairly widespread within the British Isles, its establishment on the Isle of Man is a great success story. Hen harriers began nesting here in 1977, usually in old conifer plantations. Fewer than 40 pairs are breeding here currently, but many more assemble to roost during the winter in what has become the largest communal hen harrier roost in western Europe at the Ballaugh Curraghs.

Evidence now suggests that the hen harrier is moving away from this once favoured locale, and is spreading more widely across the island.

The descending path is a pleasure to follow, flanked high up on the moors by gorse and heather. Lower down it becomes gullied and then gradually twists down along the edge of Ballakillingan Plantation before reaching and passing a row of lovely beech trees as it crosses through Skyhill Wood.

SKY HILL

'Sky Hill' is derived from *Skogarfjall*, meaning 'wooded hill'. In 1079, the Battle of Sky Hill took place on ground to the south of the Sulby–Ramsey road. The *Chronicle of the Kings of Mann and the Isles* record that a Norseman, Godred Crovan, mustered a great number of ships and came to Mann where he joined battle with King Fingal and the people of the land. Defeated twice, on the third attempt he landed his army by night at Ramsey, and hid 300 men in the woods of Sky Hill. Next day, at the height of the battle, the hidden forces attacked the Manxmen from behind and victory for Godred was assured. He treated the islanders mercifully, and established the Norse dynasty that ruled Mann until 1265. Godred is thought by some to be the 'King Orry' of Manx tradition, though others question whether the king existed at all.

The Sky Hill battle is significant in Manx lore because, although the date of the first national Tynwald cannot be ascertained, it is thought that it might have been following Godred's conquest of the island. Set against this, the island celebrated 1000 years of unbroken parliamentary rule in 1979, which clearly suggests an earlier date than Godred's battle at Sky Hill. Indeed, the establishment of the Tynwald is credited to the time when the Kingdom of the Sudreys, which comprised the Outer Hebrides and the Isle of Man, came into being, thought to be in the 970s.

The view from Sky Hill is especially agreeable. Jurby church, white-painted, stands conspicuously on the coastline, while northwards across the sea lie the hills of Galloway, including Cairnsmore of Fleet and The Merrick. The Point of Ayre lighthouse just gets in on the act, clinging to the northern tip of the island and peeping over the low-lying Bride Hills. Further east the Lakeland fells of Cumbria present familiar hills viewed from an unfamiliar angle.

The track eventually curves down to meet the A3 Sulby to Ramsey road. Cross with care, and turn right for about 500m to reach the turning into **Glen Auldyn**, where the walk ends. There are fairly regular bus services along the Sulby Glen road into Ramsey, which is little more than 1km (½ mile) further on.

WALK 10

Maughold Brooghs and Port Mooar

Start/Finish	Maughold (SC 490 917)
Distance	7.3km (4½ miles)
Height gain	290m (950ft)
Parking	Small car park on edge of village

There are many places where the Manx coastal scenery is outstanding; north of the small village of Maughold (pronounce it *Mackle't* and you'll be close), it is exceptional. This walk first explores the sea cliffs known as Maughold Brooghs, and then visits the lovely bay of Port Mooar before making a lazy return along part of the Raad ny Foillan.

Start by leaving the car park, turning right and following the road for 1.8km (a little over 1 mile), as far as a signposted path on the right to Maughold Brooghs. Along this stretch of road there are fine views left to the ridge of North Barrule and Clagh Ouyr, beyond which the summit of Snaefell can also be picked out.

The path, initially enclosed, climbs easily and breaks out into a lovely terrace walk above the inlet of **Port e Vullen**. As in many places on the island, the path is flanked by healthy stands of gorse, which in springtime bring vivid colour to the day along with their heady aroma like cinnamon and coconut.

The **coastline** of Maughold is very steep, and much-favoured by breeding birds. Here is the island's largest colony of cormorants, along with substantial numbers of kittiwake, guillemot, black guillemot, puffin, peregrine falcon, chough and raven. Out at

Following the coastal path around Maughold

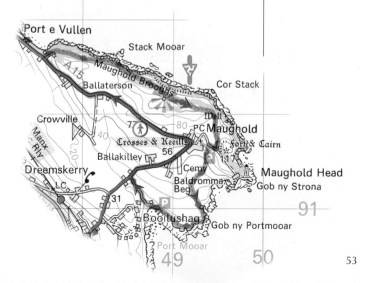

53

sea, don't be surprised to see the bobbing head of a grey seal from time to time, or a basking shark, which are known to frequent these waters.

The path steadily works a way above the sea cliffs and from a couple of ancient Scots pine climbs to a shelter and topograph from which the southern coast of Scotland and the fells of the Lake District (here called the Cumberland Hills) are visible. From the topograph, continue with a clear path that leaves the area of **Maughold Brooghs** at a gate, then following a field-side path to another gate giving onto a parking area. From here, for those that wish to visit it, a path leads left and steeply down to **St Maughold's Well**.

> **Maughold** was a native of Ulster, and by all accounts not the most Christian-living of people, having been found guilty of murder. He was brought before St Patrick, who felt unable to absolve him of his sins, and ordered that it be left in the hands of God by casting the luckless soul adrift in a coracle.
>
> With God's good grace shining upon him, Maughold eventually reached the Isle of Man where he met two men who taught him the word of God with such evident success that Maughold succeeded them as bishop. In a slight variation on this theme, St Maughold is acclaimed as the person who first brought Christianity to the island.

An optional extension here is to leave the ongoing vehicle track, and take to a steeply climbing path onto the top of Maughold Head itself.

◀ Follow the vehicle track to join a lane and here turn right towards a churchyard, wherein there is a fine collection of Manx cross slabs and, in the church, one of the earliest examples of the Triskellion, the Manx three legs emblem.

At the churchyard wall, take the lane going left and down through a gate. The ongoing track wanders down between hedgerows, embankments and low stone walls. Eventually, it reaches a couple of gates giving into fields. Go over a stile beside the left-hand one of these, and keep forward down the ensuing field to a ladder/stile at

MAUGHOLD PARISH CHURCH

Built on the site of an earlier structure, the church of St Maughold may well have been the seat of the Manx bishopric. The present church retains nothing that pre-dates the 11th century (the Irish Romanesque arch of the west doorway is thought to date from this time), although there are some lovely 13th-century windows in the south walls of the nave.

The parish church at Maughold and its graveyard form a centre of religious significance unique in the Isle of Man. The church itself is not dissimilar to other Manx churches, but the churchyard, which was the site of Maughold's Celtic monastery dating from the 7th century, contains numerous reminders of the island's Celtic and Viking past, from the oblong forms of three ancient *keeills* (chapels) to the largest single collection of cross slabs anywhere. The churchyard also contains the graves of many notable Manx people, from William Callister, founder of the Isle of Man Bank, and Robert Faragher, a radical champion of the campaign to secure the popular election of the House of Keys, to the Hall Caine Monument, a memorial to the successful Manx novelist. Within the church will be found the Maughold parish cross, a weathered work of art made from sandstone brought from the Cumbrian coast at St Bees, depicting one of the earliest forms of the Three Legs of Man. It dates from the 14th century, and is the only remaining such cross on the island. The workmanship, in spite of hundreds of years of weathering is still discernibly remarkable.

Located within the churchyard of St Maughold's, the cross-house contains the island's largest display of cross slabs, dating from the 7th century. At first glance, these are simply a collection of weathered and faded crosses housed in a shelter open to the elements. But closer inspection reveals a treasury of Celtic and Manx history, with good and clear examples of runic inscriptions. The Manx crosses are a study in themselves, and it is fitting to find so many together. Almost one-third of the pre-Norse crosses found on the island are preserved here.

the bottom. Over this go left and down to the seashore at a neat little bay, with Maughold lighthouse coming into view.

Turn right to pursue a delightful shoreline path, which keeps to a splendid line just above the water's edge and eventually turns into the larger bay of **Port Mooar**. Go towards a white shore cottage, crossing rocks and a short section of boulder beach towards the end, and then turn right up a lane, climbing to a T-junction. Turn right and walk up to the village of **Maughold**, swinging left to return to the car park. ◄

If time permits, it is worth turning into Maughold Church.

WALK 11
Cornaa and Ballaglass Glen

Start/Finish	Cornaa (SC 466 899)
Distance	7km (4¼ miles)
Height gain	215m (705ft)
Parking	Ballaglass Glen car park

Between Port Mooar, near Maughold, and Laxey, the Raad ny Foillan spends most of its time inland of the coast, only once touching on it, and that all-too-briefly at the lovely Port Cornaa. The walk down Glen Cornaa is truly beautiful, and terminates at a neat cove from where one Swedish entrepreneur had planned to export gunpowder. Alas, he failed to discuss his manufacturing plans with the Manx government, which adopted a fairly punitive attitude to the oversight.

Begin from the parking area at the north-eastern tip of the Ballaglass Glen and walk down the road, soon reaching Cornaa House in **Cornaa** and the glen's mill. Here leave the road by branching left (signed for Port Cornaa) and climbing as a stony track. This shortly links up with the **Raad ny Foillan** and goes right as a rough track. Follow this down the valley into mature woodland of beech and oak.

The 6.4ha (16 acres) of **Ballaglass Glen** were
acquired in 1952 by the Manx government, and the
area is now managed as semi-natural woodland. The
tree species consist of mature oak with beech, larch
and pine, and there's some natural regeneration of
willow, birch and ash around old mine buildings.

Ballaglass Glen was once the home of an
important corn mill, last used in 1951. It was a
typical Manx mill, with threshing facilities and drying kiln in addition to the grinding machinery. The
stone buildings found in the glen were erected by
the Great Mona Mining Company, which operated
from 1854 until 1857 and again from 1866 to 1867,
mining a vein of zinc and copper. The mine was
short-lived, typical of many mines in the days of
speculative mining in the 19th century.

Eventually the track descends to a gate giving into
riverside pasture. Here keep forward, heading for the
cove ahead. Cross a bridge spanning the Cornaa river,
and walk on, alongside a fence, to a small footbridge
near a beach cottage; the
stream that the bridge
spans if often

Beach hut, Port Cornaa

non-existent. Beyond the bridge, go left to the pebbly beach, a lovely secluded spot.

Now walk up the road that leads away from the beach. There is lovely woodland on the glenside, and although paths seem to run through it, they are not rights-of-way. Fortunately, the road is generally quiet: mosses grow on top of the walls and wood sorrel and pink purslane are dominant along the road margins, birds fill the hedgerows with song and the heady scent of wild ransoms lies heavily on the air.

Follow the road until another appears obliquely from the right, at a ford. Here cross a nearby footbridge and go forward onto a signposted path for **Glen Mona**. The track is initially stony, climbing beside a stream and then between steep embankments before wandering on agreeably through a narrow wooded glen.

Climb steadily to meet and cross the Manx Electric Railway (take care here, and listen for trams). Then continue in the same direction, to emerge onto the main Laxey–Ramsey road, opposite the Glen Mona Hotel. Turn right and walk along the roadside footpath for about 800m and then leave it at a cottage (Hill Crest) by turning right onto a signed track, soon crossing the railway again, and this time by a bridge. A lovely, gorsey track now ensues, taking the route through a few twists and turns. When it forks at a footpath signpost, keep left, and continue to follow the main thrust of the track, which finally reaches the edge of **Ballaglass Glen**.

Cross the immediate track and go down steps to emerge at the Ballaglass Glen Railway Station. Turn immediately right here to re-enter the glen. More steps lead down to a footbridge spanning the glen river. When the path forks, near an old building, bear right.

The path shortly descends to run above the glen's river again, but, just after passing a riverside picnic area, climb to the left, away from the river, to intercept another track, descending to the right. Turn onto this and follow it downriver to emerge on the Port Cornaa road at Cornaa House and the old mill. Turn left here, and walk back up the road to the parking area and starting point.

WALK 12
Dhoon Glen

Start/Finish	A2 road bend at Dhoon (SC 452 863)
Distance	2.25km (1½ miles)
Height gain	190m (625ft)
Refreshments	Small refreshment kiosk at start
Parking	At start

The brevity of this walk should not lull anyone into thinking it is nothing more than a quick dash; the scenery within this wooded glen is superb, graced as it is by a tumbling waterfall that spills from pool to pool as it cascades seawards. Just taking all this in is time consuming in itself – as it should be – while those interested in birdlife and flora will find much to divert their attentions.

There is a sizeable parking area at a roadbend, opposite the Dhoon Glen halt on the Manx Electric Railway.

Cross the road, bearing right, then cross the railway line to start down a narrow side lane. Before long, at a signpost, a path branches right into the head of the glen; in fact there are two paths signed at this point. Take that on the left, into the glen, and soon abandon an obvious path maintaining a level course in favour of a narrower path that descends, left, into woodland and soon reaches the course of the stream.

Dhoon Glen is one of the steepest glens on the island, running through a densely wooded valley that follows its stream to the shore. The main path meanders through a canopy of ash, wych elm, alder, sycamore, birch and mountain ash. The waterfall, half way down the valley, is known as the *Inneen Vooar*, or 'Big Girl', and is one of the highest on the island, falling over 40m (130ft). During the late 19th century, a small passenger ship, the Manx Fairy, used to run daily between Douglas and Ramsey calling at Dhoon bay to unload passengers, who spent the day on the stony beach or in the glen before making the return journey.

The descending path is clear throughout, making use of a great many steps (apparently 190 in all) linked by short, level sections, one of which leads to the remains of old mine workings, the wheelcase and chimney of which are still in good order. ◄

The mine searched for lead and zinc, most notably during the 19th century, but was not especially successful.

Onward, more steps lead towards the cascading stream and, in due course, the upper section of its **waterfall**, after which the gradient relaxes a little before running on to a small viewpoint directly above the stony beach, which is easily accessed.

On the way down to the beach, a branching path, on the right, will have been passed. The return journey makes use of this, rising all the while at a gentle gradient, first heading south above the coast, and then doubling back before swinging to the west as it steadily climbs out of the glen to rejoin the narrow lane used at the start of the walk.

The shoreline of Dhoon Glen

WALK 13

Clagh Ouyr and North Barrule

Start/Finish	Black Hut (SC 406 885)
Distance	9.5km (6 miles)
Height gain	505m (1657ft)
Parking	At start (limited)

North Barrule, dominating the coastal town of Ramsey, is the second-highest hill on the island and its shapely summit is a distinctive feature. There is a steep and rugged ascent from The Hibernian, near Ramsey, but a much less strenuous ascent can be made from the Black Hut, below Snaefell, high on the TT Course. The going can be soft underfoot, but only in patches, and the return dips into the Cornaa valley.

Cross the road with care: at all times of the year there are motorcyclists and motorists of varying ability who like to test their skills, and your nerves, on this upland part of the TT Course. Go over a step/stile beside a gate (signpost), descending a little before climbing alongside a wall to another signpost at a wall corner. From the wall corner go left, still alongside a wall for about 100m, and then strike upwards to the right on a clear path, to the ridge above, and then pulling easily onto the first top, **Clagh Ouyr**. North Barrule now lies 4km (2½ miles) away, with the route lying across two minor, unnamed summits on the way. ◄

In places the terrain is boggy, but this can be avoided in all but the worst weather.

Clagh Ouyr and North Barrule from the summit of nearby Snaefell

As you approach North Barrule, a wall stands before the final steep pull to the summit, a stunning viewpoint embracing the whole of the northern part of the island, and, on the distant horizons, the fells of the English

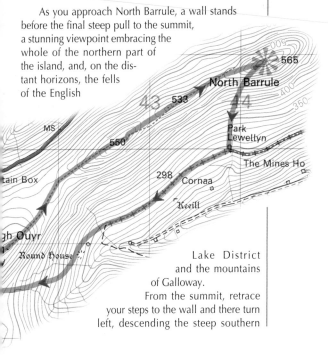

Lake District and the mountains of Galloway.

From the summit, retrace your steps to the wall and there turn left, descending the steep southern

63

flank of the mountain into the Cornaa valley, aiming for the ruins of **Park Llewellyn Farm** (SC 439 900).

At the ruins, turn right on a broad track heading up the valley, keeping an eye open for the walled St Mary's Church (*Keeil Noo Voirrey*) lower down on the left. Continue heading up the valley, steadily rising now, to a small building and sheep enclosures. Clagh Ouyr is now ahead and slightly to the right as the track dwindles to a path and then peters out altogether. Climbing more steeply now, aim to the south of Clagh Ouyr, to avoid needless ascent. Strong walkers can more or less head upwards to meet the outward route, but otherwise a course around the southern end of the hill will be easier to maintain.

Once on the lower, southern slopes of Clagh Ouyr, it is simply a matter of heading downhill in the direction of the **Black Hut**. A final, gentle uphill stretch leads to the road and the end of the walk.

WALK 14

Snaefell from the Bungalow

Start/Finish	Bungalow (SC 396 868)
Distance	6.8km (4½ miles)
Height gain	405m (1329ft)
Refreshments	Summit (seasonal)
Parking	At start

The highest part of a country has always drawn attention, for a variety of reasons, not all of them good. The top of Snaefell is no exception, and the desire of Victorians to look down on the island led to the building of the Snaefell Mountain Railway to transport them to the top without undue fatigue. Modern communications have also imposed a tariff, cluttering the summit with man-made paraphernalia. Sadly, it is the ability to ride to the summit and have a cup of tea and a scone (delicious, by the way) that makes Snaefell interesting, for without these trappings this would simply be another fundamentally uninteresting hill, the highest of five Marilyns on the island.

Snaefell from Beinn-y-Phott

Just beyond the road junction and mountain railway crossing point, high on the Ramsey to Douglas road, a gate on the left gives onto a steadily rising footpath that leads unerringly to the summit café less than a mile distant. Keep to the right of the building to locate a concrete walkway heading towards a radio mast, and leave this when convenient to walk across to the summit trig and topograph.

The **Snaefell Mountain Railway** celebrated its centenary in 1995, and it still operates with its six original tramcars, the only electric mountain railway in the British Isles. With gradients as steep as 1:12 in places, there is a central 'Fell' rail which helps the cars to break. It is 8.8km

(5½ miles) from base to summit and construction of the 3ft 6in (107cm) gauge track was begun in January 1895. It opened to the public barely seven months later, on 21 August 1895. Today the line operates from the end of April to late September.

Walkers who do not want to experience the rigours of the tussock moorland to the north of the summit, should simply retreat the way they came. Otherwise set off from the summit, roughly following grid north, targeting a small plantation at SC 396 902.

The terrain is untracked but generally easy if occasionally wet, and populated by a few **moorland birds** – meadow pipit, grouse and curlew – as well as mountain hare. Hen harriers, peregrine, long- and short-eared owls also feature here.

The objective is to locate a signpost for the Millennium Way near the top of the valley leading north-west to the Block Eary Reservoir. Once this has been found, turn left on an indistinct trod across the moorland, indistinct but improving, after a while, once the next signpost has been reached. Thereafter it scampers agreeably across the north-west shoulder of Snaefell, reaching the Sulby Glen road a little less than 1.6km (1 mile) from the Bungalow. Turn left and follow the roadside verge back to the start.

WALK 15

Laxey, Agneash and King Orry's Grave

Start/Finish	Laxey (SC 433 847)
Distance	6.8km (4½ miles)
Height gain	260m (853ft)
Refreshments	At Laxey and near Laxey Wheel turning
Parking	Laxey

It will require only a short diversion from this route to visit the renowned Laxey waterwheel, but it is well worth the effort just to see this remaining monument to Manx mining industry. Otherwise, the route wanders steeply up to the lovely white-cottaged village of Agneash before looping across country to connect with the coastal path and a visit to King Orry's Grave.

Begin from the car park along the road to Laxey Wheel and walk up the road, passing the tourist information centre and gift shop, and then immediately branching right on a descending lane to the fire station. Just before the fire station, cross a footbridge spanning the Mooar River and follow an enclosed path up to a road just below the **Laxey Wheel** car park.

Famed afar as the largest waterwheel in the world, **the Laxey Wheel**, or Lady Isabella (named after the then Governor's wife),

was built in 1854, at a time when the Manx mining industry was in its heyday. The purpose of the wheel was to pump water from the lead mines. It has a circumference of 84m (276ft), a diameter of 23m (75ft), and is capable of lifting 1140 litres (251 gallons) of water per minute from mines more than 330m (1083ft) deep.

The Laxey mines were originally opened in 1750 and were entered from surface adits rather than shafts. They were enormously productive and proved a steady investment. By the 1850s an initial £80 share had risen in value to over £1000, an impressive return for a lead mine by the standards of the day.

Having visited the wheel, go down steps beside the road and descend to a road bridge (on the left). Here, turn right up the road to **Agneash**.

Walk all the way up to Agneash, climbing steeply. Once there, leave the road, as it bends left, by branching right, near Hillside Cottage and a cottage called The Orchids, onto a signed footpath descending steps. This becomes enclosed as it heads for the Glen Agneash burn and is crossed by a wooden footbridge, with more steps beyond it.

There's a fine view backwards at this point, over the village of Agneash, set against a fine backdrop of the Laxey Glen and Snaefell.

At the top of the steps, turn right on a grassy footpath to a gate, and follow the ensuing path as it rises gently through gorse and climbs past a ruined building. ◄

The path climbs to a kissing-gate and from there goes forward as a broad grassy track across the centre of a sloping pasture to a gate in the top corner. Over a stile beside the gate, bear right alongside a fence to a step/stile giving onto a gorse-enclosed footpath, which leads up to pass behind a row of cottages. From the rear corner, keep left onto a narrow grassy path heading for a distant farm building, which leads to a ladder/stile giving onto a broad track bearing right, through a small plantation.

Keep following the track to a T-junction, turn right and, 30m later, go left through a gate and onto a broad enclosed track that leads up to a farm. A step/stile crosses a fence, beyond which a path runs behind farm buildings to a metal gate giving out onto a farm lane. Turn left and walk out to a T-junction.

The countryside here, undulating, patterned by gorse hedgerows, is especially beautiful and much favoured by patrolling hen harriers, kestrels and short-eared owls.

At the T-junction, turn right and eventually emerge on the **B11** secondary road, shared by the coastal path. Turn right and follow the road for almost 2km (1¼ miles) to reach the site of **King Orry's Grave**, a dissected site with the remnants of the grave on either side of the road, well worth taking a few moments to visit.

KING ORRY'S GRAVE

These are the remains of a prehistoric chambered tomb, built and used by a community of farmers about 5000 years ago. The tomb, a long barrow of complex design, consisted of a line of stone-built chambers buried under a cairn of earth and stones. There were at least three chambers beyond the entrance and they were roofed with stone slabs and covered over to create the cairn. The chambers would have been filled with burials, starting with the farthest. When excavated, few remains had survived, save one small piece of earthenware, similar to other pieces found at the Meayll circle near Cregneash. Access to the tomb would have taken place during commemorative ceremonies and the passage into the tomb and between the chambers would have been intentionally difficult to reinforce the division between the living world and the afterlife.

Today the site is in two parts, split by the road. If, as is supposed, the two halves are of the same tomb, then it was indeed both complex and large. For two centuries, a tradition persisted that the two parts were connected, but clear evidence has been obscured by the construction of the road and cottages. The grave was abandoned during the Neolithic period and since then the blocks above the entrance have collapsed.

King Orry – Godred Crovan – is a semi-legendary character revered by the Manx as their greatest king. He reigned from 1079 and created the kingdom of Mann and the Isles, stretching from the Irish Sea to the Outer Hebrides. Although numerous monuments are named in deference to him, there is no connection between the historical figure and these prehistoric remains. King Orry is believed to lie buried on the Scottish island of Islay.

King Orry's grave: a prehistoric chambered tomb

Continue a short distance farther down the road to another T-junction, this time with the A2, and there turn right towards **Laxey**. After about 200m, leave the roadside footpath by turning left onto a steeply descending concrete path that leads to a crossing point on the Manx Electric Railway. Continue on the other side, now through a narrow neck of woodland, and walk down to a lane junction beside the valley river. Turn right, go forward past a bridge and keep on past a retirement home.

Deriving its name from *laxa*, the Norse for salmon river, **Laxey**, until the 18th century, was little more than a huddle of fishermen's cottages along the coast between Douglas and Ramsey. Once mineral deposits were discovered, however, a new village was built higher up the glen, largely to accommodate the 600 men who came to work the mines. By 1857 the mines here were the principal source of zinc in the British Isles, and also produced a quantity of lead ore containing silver. Following a steady decline towards the end of the 19th century, the mines finally closed in 1929.

Beyond the retirement home turn left, crossing a footbridge and climbing on the other side to a lane. Turn right and walk up to the main road, crossing it with care to return to the starting point.

WALK 16

The Snaefell Mines

Start/Finish	Laxey (SC 434 847)
Distance	9km (5½ miles)
Height gain	280m (920ft)
Refreshments	Laxey
Parking	Laxey

This is an out-and-back walk to the derelict Snaefell Mines, beginning with a steep and steady climb to the hillside village of Agneash. Lying in the shadow of Snaefell the mines are today a reminder of a terrible disaster. They lie well off the beaten track, forgotten and rarely visited. The site is the highest major mine on the island.

The walk begins anywhere in Laxey, following the road as if heading for the **Laxey Wheel**, from where it continues up the road to the higher village of Agneash. In Agneash, bear left along a surfaced lane (SC 431 860 – the first lane on the left) – a Greenway Road. This leads out of the village, and shortly passes Ballayolgane Farm, beyond which the road surfacing ends and a rough track takes over. On the opposite side of the valley, the course of the **Snaefell Mountain Railway** can easily be picked out, carving a route up to the road crossing at the Bungalow.

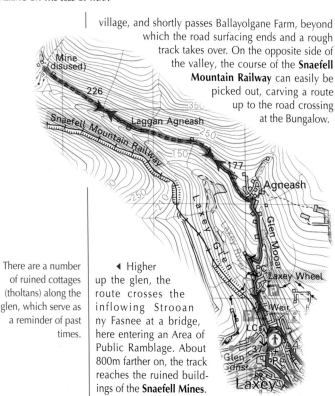

There are a number of ruined cottages (tholtans) along the glen, which serve as a reminder of past times.

◀ Higher up the glen, the route crosses the inflowing Strooan ny Fasnee at a bridge, here entering an Area of Public Ramblage. About 800m farther on, the track reaches the ruined buildings of the **Snaefell Mines**.

The **Snaefell Mines** were operated between 1856 and 1908, producing lead and zinc. Further attempts at extracting ore were made in the 1950s, but eventually the mine ceased operation. Inevitably, with this type of mining, there was loss of life, the worst event occurring in May 1897, when 20 miners were lost.

To return to Laxey, simply retrace the outward route.

WALK 17

Groudle Glen and Baldrine

Start/Finish	Groudle Glen (SC 420 782)
Distance	10km (6½ miles)
Height gain	200m (655ft)
Refreshments	Pub at Halfway House and in Baldrine
Parking	Groudle Glen

This lasso-shaped walk includes a diversion to visit the isolated St Lonan's Church and the magnificent wheel-headed cross in the graveyard. A fair measure of minor road walking makes for speedy progress, but does nothing to detract from the walk, which, in the main, passes through farming land.

From the parking area, cross a footbridge at the seaward end of the parking area, and go up steps, part of the Raad ny Foillan. Follow the path up to reach and cross the **Groudle Glen** railway line. Go forward, immediately passing a lime kiln.

> Pronounced to rhyme with 'how', **Groudle Glen** is a neat, narrow nook on the boundary between Onchan and Lonan. Until 1962 the glen had a narrow gauge railway, opened in 1896 as a holiday attraction serving a number of entertainments in the glen. Work on reconstructing the railway began in 1982, and today it is fully restored and operated seasonally by a group of volunteers.

The route soon becomes a delightful, hedgerowed track ascending gently and flanked by sycamore, ivy and bluebells, and runs on to meet a surfaced lane at a gate. Keep forward and continue up the lane until you reach the turning to **St Lonan's Church**. Here, divert right on a side lane (to St Adamnan's Church: Lonan Old Church) to visit the church, and then retrace the route and turn right onto the original line.

ST LONAN'S CHURCH

Curiously, this lovely old church isn't dedicated to St Lonan at all, but to St Adamnan, renowned biographer of St Columba, although he was also believed to be known by the name Onan. So Lonan may be a corruption of *Keeill Onan*, 'the cell or chapel of Onan'. Other authorities think the parish of Lonan is named after the third Bishop of Sodor and Man, a nephew of St Patrick, or that it was named after the Donegal saint, Lonan Machaisre.

Although part of the church is in ruins, the eastern end was restored at the end of the 19th century. The church is one of the island's oldest, some parts dating from the 12th century, and it stands on a site that was occupied by the earliest Christian missionaries. The first *keeill* was probably built on this site in the 5th century by travelling monks: it stood on the main pack-horse route from Douglas to the north of the island. Originally, the chapel was known as Keeill-ny-Traie ('The Chapel by the Shore'), and served the surrounding quarterland farms at Baldromma, Ballacreggan, Ballameanagh, Ballavarane and the farm it stands on, Ballakilley. Almost certainly this early structure would have been destroyed by the Vikings and later rebuilt. In the 12th century Reginald, King of Man, granted land at Escadalla, which included Keeill-ny-Traie, to the Prior at St Bees in Cumberland. The monks there, having more than an eye for the main chance, quickly realised the importance of the chapel's location and rebuilt it to meet their needs. It is part of their building that now remains.

When the Vikings were finally vanquished, at the Battle of Largs in 1263, the Isle of Man for a while belonged to Scotland, but soon passed to England. It was at this time that the parish system was introduced to the island and Keeill-ny-Traie became the parish church, dedicated to St Adamnan. And so it remained until the 18th century, when the parishioners complained about the church's inconvenient location at the southern edge of their parish. It took 100 years before a new church was finally

The Lonan Stone: a rare example

built at Boilley Veen, although this, too, was remote. The Act of Tynwald sanctioning the building of the new church also required the demolition of the old one, an instruction that, thankfully, was ignored: even so, the old church fell into disrepair. That part of the church is in serviceable condition today is largely thanks to the Reverend John Quinne, vicar of Lonan from 1895, who initiated the restoration of the church.

A spectacular wheel-headed cross known as the Lonan Stone stands in the graveyard of Old Lonan Church, quite probably still in its original position, reclining gently to one side in its old age. It dates from the 9th or 10th centuries, and is by far the most attractive of the Manx crosses. The decoration consists entirely of Celtic interlacing, knots and plaits. There are other crosses in a small shelter within the churchyard.

About 300m beyond the turning to St Lonan's Church, leave the road by turning left onto a signed concrete track (SC 425 798) heading towards a farm. Follow this until it runs out to meet **The Manx Electric Railway** and then the A2. Turn left along the A2, and walk as far as the Liverpool Arms **pub**, there turning right onto a side road.

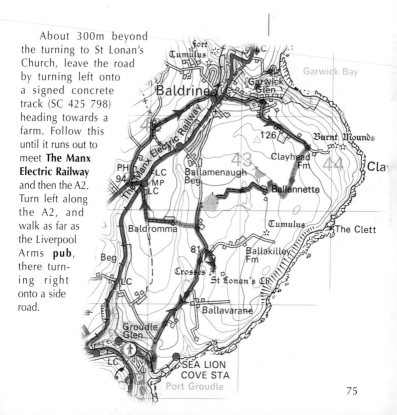

75

Continue up the lane to the entrance to Harrison Farm/Bayr House, and here turn right onto a rough track, then almost immediately bear left onto a slightly narrower track, flanked by gorse. Keep following the track until it reaches a road on the edge of **Baldrine**, and there turn right. Cross the electric railway again and go forward to a road junction. Turn left and walk downhill on a roadside footpath, and then take the next turning on the right into Clay Head Road.

Keep following the road to reach a double gate at the entrance to **Clayhead Farm**. Go through this and continue walking for about 50m and then turn right on a signed footpath over a stile beside a gate. Stay along the right-hand edge of the ensuing field to reach a ladder/ stile. Over this bear left along an enclosed track. Keep following the track, which eventually finds a way round to a group of farm buildings at the Ballannette Nature Reserve, and then continue beyond it on a concrete vehicle track, heading towards a group of lakes.

> **Ballannette** is a natural wetlands area sensitively developed to avoid disturbance of native and visiting birdlife. Ballannette is farmed using environmental and ecological methods that include a ban on the use of chemicals. Fields are cut for hay as late as possible each year so as not to affect nesting birds. Over 120 species of wild flowers have been identified in the region. Since 1997 hundreds of trees and shrubs have been planted; some of which are now able to sustain tree-nesting birdlife.
>
> Many species of birds and insects are found at Ballannette, such as chough, lapwing, tufted duck and snipe.

Eventually the track comes out onto a lane. Turn left and soon rejoin the outward route of the walk near **St Lonan's Church**. Now retrace your steps back to Groudle Glen. Just on recrossing the Groudle Glen railway line, turn right onto a gently descending path that leads down to the inland end of the parking area.

WALK 18

Crosby, Baldwin and Union Mills

Start/Finish	Old Church Road, Crosby (SC 326 793)
Distance	13km (8 miles)
Height gain	268m (880ft)
Refreshments	pubs in Crosby and Union Mills
Parking	Roadside parking along Old Church Road, Crosby

Visiting three ancient settlements, this tour of the farmlands north of the River Dhoo begins along a stretch of the Millennium Way and then uses fields to reach Baldwin, before making good use of old lanes to return to Union Mills from where the old Douglas to Peel railway trackbed provides an easy means of return to Crosby.

Walk up Old Church Road in Crosby to the main road (**A1**) and cross with care into narrow Eyreton Road opposite. The route is signed as part of the Millennium Way, which indeed it is, as far as Baldwin.

Continue climbing up Eyreton Road until it swings to the right, and here (SC 332 801) leave it by going forward and ascending a rough stony track between walls, with a fine view half-left of Greeba Mountain and Slieau

Slieau Ruy and Greeba Mountain from the Millennium Way

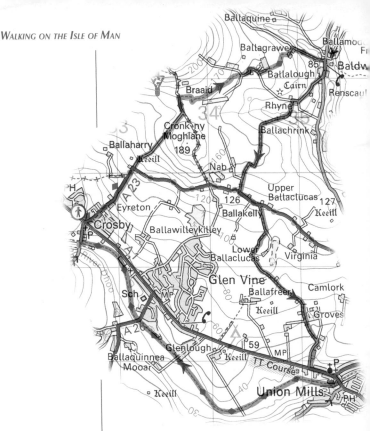

In the middle of the field on the left, note the fenced site of St Bridget's Chapel (Keeill Vreeshey), an early Christian chapel site.

Ruy (Walk 19). ◄ Carry on up the track to a junction and there turn left for a little over 100m to a Millennium Way signpost, there leaving the lane at a kissing-gate for a field-edge path.

Keep to the field edge and follow this to a through-stile (signpost). Over this, go forward along another field edge, but then leave the field after about 100m, by bearing right over another stile. In the ensuing pasture, again keep to the field headland, following this round to a stile beside a signpost. A large pasture now follows. Keep forward along the left-hand edge. At a gate on the far side of the field, go through onto a farm access.

The track runs on to the edge of **Ballalough** Farm. Here go forward to a footpath signpost and turn left, over a stile and kissing-gate (Millennium waymark just over the stile). Continue along the field edge to stiles spanning a fence, one either side of a field track. Now go straight across the next pasture to cross another fence, a track and ladder/stile.

Cross another field and on the other side turn right towards **Ballagrawe**, from where its access leads downhill to Annie's Cottage (signed 'Millennium Way FP152') and a right turn towards **Baldwin**, finally meeting the village road at a T-junction.

Turn right for 200m and then leave the main road for an ascending lane, a bridleway, on the right. Follow the lane past The Rhyne and, a short way further on, leave the surfaced lane by turning left at a signpost onto another stony track flanked by overgrown walls.

The descending track treks between farm fields for some distance before finally coming down to meet the Crosby–Mount Rule road. Turn left and, after about 300m, turn right at a lane between established hedgerows of gorse and hawthorn. After 350m bear right towards a metal gate, continuing on a hedgerowed lane (Trollaby Lane). Keep on down the lane to meet the A1 main road, and there turn left towards **Union Mills**.

The village of **Union Mills** was known from 1511 as Mullin Doway ('The Mill on the Black Ford)', and in the middle of the 17th century Mullin Oates. In 1807 a cloth mill was added to the original corn mill by local entrepreneur William Kelly. The new company was called Flail and Fleece United and the company issued card money with the inscription 'I promise to pay the Bearer on demand Five Shillings British. (Wm. Kelly) Union Mills (4 Sept. 1811).' This was a common practice at the time: from 1805 to 1817 the lack of copper and silver coins circulating on the island meant that many merchants issued their own money in the form of engraved cards of various shapes and sizes.

The Isle of Man
Steam Railway
Douglas to Peel line
started in July 1873
and was the first
railway line on the
Isle of Man.

Only a few walls remain of the original mill but the millhouse still stands in the village. The post office at Union Mills also has an interesting connection: the Gibb family, some of whom eventually turned into the musical band the Bee Gees, lived here before moving to Manchester and then Australia.

Just after a garage and near a road junction, cross the main road with care and, just before the bridge spanning the River Dhoo, turn right into a small industrial estate. At the far side of the estate a gate gives onto the trackbed of the Douglas to Peel railway line (the Heritage Trail). ◄

Turn right onto this and now follow the trackbed for 4km (2½ miles), crossing the road up to Glen Vine at a derelict gatehouse and continuing, the trackbed now surfaced, to the next gatehouse near the site of the former Crosby Station. Here turn right to return to the start. The trackbed passes through an extensive area of wetland (known as *curragh*), which is a good place to keep an eye open for birdlife and wild flowers.

WALK 19
Slieau Ruy and Greeba Mountain

Start/Finish	Old Church Road, Crosby (SC 326 793)
Distance	12km (7½ miles)
Height gain	460m (1510ft)
Refreshments	pubs in Crosby and Union Mills
Parking	Roadside parking along Old Church Road, Crosby

The first part of this walk follows Walk 18, using a section of the Millennium Way before bearing off to climb onto Slieau Roy and its lower satellite, Greeba Mountain. Although both summits lie within the Area of Public Ramblage, they are not often visited and the terrain is potentially confusing, making this walk unsuitable for days of poor visibility. On a clear day, however, the prospect offered by this energetic circuit is excellent.

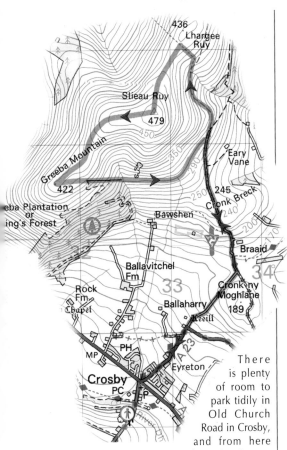

There is plenty of room to park tidily in Old Church Road in Crosby, and from here walk out to the main road, crossing with care into Eyreton Road. ▸ Continue up the road until it swings to the right (SC 332 801), and here leave it by going forward onto a rough stony track rising between walls. Carry on up the track to a junction, and there turn left.

Shortly, leave the Millennium Way (which crosses into an adjacent field) and keep forward to pass **Braaid** Farm, beyond which the lane becomes steeper and quite

The route is signposted as part of the Millennium Way.

81

A stony track rises between walls, part of the Millennium Way

rough underfoot. Go past the turning to Bawshen and continue uphill (signed for Little London), eventually passing the track down to the ruins of **Eary Vane** Farm. At a cattle grid the route reaches the edge of an Area of Public Ramblage, and continues roughly northwards, but bearing left to cross the top of a stream gully. Slieau Ruy now lies to the south-west.

Keep on to a path junction (signpost for Rhenass) and there turn abruptly left heading for the summit of **Slieau Ruy**, the top of which is marked by a trig pillar and cairn. There is an outstanding view from the summit, and the surprise is that the hill is not more popular.

Continue now by following the lie of the land heading for Greeba Mountain (it is not a direct line, although one is almost possible). By keeping to the highest ground between the two summits, albeit boggy at some times of year, the top of **Greeba Mountain** is soon reached. Fine views also wait here, for this is one of the best vantage points on the island.

From the top of Greeba Mountain head eastwards to intercept a wall at the top boundary of Greeba Plantation, then maintain an easterly direction along the plantation boundary to reach a stream at its easterly edge. Cross the stream and now contour east and north-east, following a wall along the boundary of the Area of Public Ramblage. This leads back to the cattle grid crossed on the outward leg. Here turn right and retrace the walk back to Crosby.

THE SOUTH

All that remains of the once-extensive Rushen Abbey (Walk 37)

WALK 20

Peel Hill and Corrins Hill

Start/Finish	Fenella Beach car park (SC 241 843)
Distance	6.4km (4 miles)
Height gain	260m (853ft)
Refreshments	Café on breakwater, and numerous places in Peel
Parking	At start

This short walk over the twin-topped hill that dominates the harbour town of Peel, and to a good extent protects it from south-westerlies, is quite exhilarating and, after an energetic beginning, soon takes to the seaward side of the hill before scampering to the highest point and then winding down to the inland valley road. The views are outstanding and embrace southern Scotland and the Mountains of Mourne in Northern Ireland.

Considered by many to be the most 'Manx' of the island's towns, **Peel**, including the historic St Patrick's Isle, is an ideal town to explore, full of narrow lanes with buildings of character and indeterminate history. All roads here lead to the harbour,

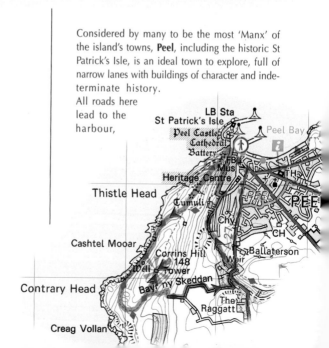

emphasising the town's importance, then and now, as a centre for the Manx fishing industry. Visitors to Peel should seek out the award-winning House of Manannan, adjacent to the harbour, a perfect place to learn about the history of the Isle of Man from the earliest settlers to the present day.

Leave the car park and climb immediately, right, onto a broad, gravel track rising onto Peel Hill. There are a number of tracks and cross-tracks on the ascent, but the simplest thing to do is keep going up, to reach the top of Peel Hill. Then maintain the same direction over the hill and down to an obvious col between Peel Hill and the more southerly Corrins Hill. Here, at the col, the Raad ny Foillan (the coastal path) crosses in the form of a broad grassy path. Bear right onto this for a spectacular terraced walk high above the sea cliffs of **Cashtal Mooar**. This spins along in delightful fashion and, near Contrary Head, it divides. Keep left, gradually rounding the southern end of Corrins Hill and starting to head back towards Peel.

You leave the Raad ny Foillan at this point (which dashes off to the right). Instead, keep left, walking alongside a wall. At this point it is an easy scamper up to the top of **Corrins Hill**, which is well worth the little extra effort for the view alone.

Return to the wall and when this bears right go with it, descending to a ladder/stile giving onto a short lane leading down to a farmhouse. At the farmhouse, turn left onto a broad track, and then follow an obvious course winding down to meet a road. Turn left, almost immediately crossing a road bridge (take care against approaching traffic here), and, on the other side, turn right down wooden steps (signpost) to meet the River Neb near an old watermill.

Here, double back left to go under the road bridge, now on the course of an old railway trackbed that guides you back to the outskirts of Peel. But, a short way from the road bridge, bear left towards the river for a pleasant footpath, finally reaching the end of the elongated

Peel Castle and grounds | Peel harbour at another road bridge. Cross the bridge and follow the road towards **Peel Castle** and the start of the walk.

PEEL CASTLE

The castle of Peel Island was built by William le Scrope, King of Mann from 1392 until 1399, who later became Earl of Wiltshire and treasurer to Richard II. Ostensibly the castle was built to defend the cathedral here, which had been sacked by the Earl of Galloway in 1388. The castle is simple in design, consisting of a fortified gateway and a keep – quite a barrier if you imagine the modern causeway to be no longer there – with a red sandstone curtain wall.

For his support of Richard II, Scrope paid with his life at the hands of Henry IV, who gave the island to Henry Percy, Duke of Northumberland. But the Percys rebelled against Henry and after their defeat in 1403 the island was given to the first of the Stanleys, Sir John, for life, later confirmed in perpetuity, although Sir John never actually visited the island. But the move in effect brought the uneasy days of Manx history to a close. The Stanley family ruled as the Kings of Mann for 350 years.

WALK 21

St John's, Patrick and the Heritage Trail

Start/Finish	St John's (SC 277 816)
Distance	11./km (7¼ miles)
Height gain	312m (1024ft)
Refreshments	Pubs in St John's, or a wider choice in Peel
Parking	Car park at old railway station, next to St John's Primary School

This walk combines ancient routes of different kinds – railway and trade – but its real purpose is to wander across the gorse-decked flanks of Slieau Whallian. It begins not far from Tynwald Hill, to which everyone should make a short detour to visit the Royal Chapel of St John the Baptist. Once beyond the Slieau Whallian Plantation, the route romps up to cross the south-western shoulder of the hill before plunging down to Kirk Patrick. The return is along a stretch of the Heritage Trail, the reincarnation of the route of the now defunct Isle of Man Railway between Douglas and Peel.

ROYAL CHAPEL OF ST JOHN THE BAPTIST

Not only is the church the parish church of the village of St John's, it is also the National Civic Church for the island, the 'Tynwald Church'. On Tynwald Day the church performs two functions. It is, of course, the consecrated building used for the religious element of the day, but later it also acts as a court house. The present church was built by Richard and Benjamin Lane of Manchester in the 13th-century style known as English Transitional. It is faced with granite from South Barrule quarry, but also uses stone from Ballavar, with chancel steps in Poyllvaaish marble.

Little is known about the early history of this site, but it is probable that there has been a place of worship here or hereabouts since the 10th century. Evidence for this comes in the form of a runic cross – Osruth's Cross – dating from AD950 and unearthed when the earlier cross-shaped church, dating from 1699, was demolished in 1847. The cross stands in the porch of the present church.

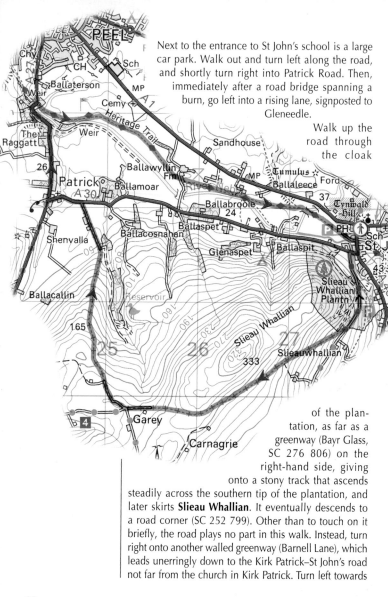

Next to the entrance to St John's school is a large car park. Walk out and turn left along the road, and shortly turn right into Patrick Road. Then, immediately after a road bridge spanning a burn, go left into a rising lane, signposted to Gleneedle.

Walk up the road through the cloak of the plantation, as far as a greenway (Bayr Glass, SC 276 806) on the right-hand side, giving onto a stony track that ascends steadily across the southern tip of the plantation, and later skirts **Slieau Whallian**. It eventually descends to a road corner (SC 252 799). Other than to touch on it briefly, the road plays no part in this walk. Instead, turn right onto another walled greenway (Barnell Lane), which leads unerringly down to the Kirk Patrick–St John's road not far from the church in Kirk Patrick. Turn left towards the church, and go past it to a T-junction, there turning right, towards Peel.

After about 1km (½ mile) the road dinks across a road bridge. Just on crossing the bridge, turn right down wooden steps to meet the River Neb near an old watermill. Here the route joins the Heritage Trail, and this flower-flanked old trackbed can be followed, right, for about 4km (2½ miles) back to St John's.

Although not directly on the route, it is worth deviating at the end to walk up to inspect **Tynwald Hill**, a location of considerable important to the island and its people. ▸

St John's is not unique in having an outdoor Tynwald: others have been held at Cronk Urleigh, near Kirk Michael, and at Cronk Keeill Abban, near St Luke's Church north of Baldwin.

TYNWALD HILL

Tynwald Hill: ceremonial 'Thing' site

Said to be composed of earth gathered from the 17 parishes on the island, and so representing the whole island, Tynwald Hill is a man-made four-tiered mound adjoining the road at St John's, and the focal point of the island's legislature, representing, as it does, an unbroken tradition of a parliamentary assembly in the Isle of Man more than a thousand years old. There is some suggestion that the site of Tynwald Hill marks the spot of an ancient burial mound.

The name 'Tynwald' is derived from the Norse language, in which a 'thing' is an assembly or meeting, and *vollr*, a field. Before Parliaments and High Courts there were 'Things', an early system of justice and administration. The original principles of the ancient Thing-*vollr* are still the basis of the Manx constitution today. Normally, the Court of Tynwald meets throughout the year in Douglas, on the third Tuesday of each month, but annually, on the Old Midsummer's Day (5th July), the monarch (represented by the Lieutenant-Governor), the High Court Judges (known as Deemsters), the elected members of the House of Keys (the Lower House and the equivalent of the British House of Commons), the appointed members of the Legislative Council (the Upper House), and a number of civic authorities meet to give effect to the island's laws, proclaiming them in both English and Manx. The occasion is the only time in the year when the West Door of St John's Church is opened, to access the processional way that leads directly from the church to Tynwald Hill, a distance of 110m.

WALK 22
Glen Maye, the coast path and Patrick

Start/Finish	Glen Maye (SC 235 798)
Distance	11km (6¾ miles)
Height gain	430m (1410ft)
Refreshments	Waterfall Country Hotel
Parking	Car park at head of Glen Maye

This delightful walk begins by heading north along the coastal path before diving inland to visit to the small village of Kirk Patrick and its Church of the Holy Trinity. An ancient greenway then leads across upland pastures before returning along a quiet lane to Glen Maye.

From the Glen Maye car park, go down steps into the top end of the glen and soon cross a bridge above the waterfall. Take the steps descending to the base of the waterfall and then continue on a riverside path. Lower down the glen, at a path junction, remain with the riverside path to reach the remains of a waterwheel. Here, leave the glen by turning up to a gate.

The route crosses the glen road at this point, but if time allows it is worth taking a stroll down the glen to the coast; it is quite a special place, from which a path climbs very steeply to join the main route above. It is easier, however, to walk back up the glen and go up a signed path, which here is both the **Raad ny Foillan** and the **Bayr ny Skeddan**. The path climbs briefly and, not far above

the bay, branches. Bear right, as the path then adopts a superb line across the top of cliffs and headlands, constantly undulating and changing direction in a way that makes the walk invigorating and encouraging.

The rocky foreshore at Glen Maye

> A pair of **binoculars** would be useful on this walk, as the cliffs are popular with a whole range of birds from the fairly commonplace herring gull, to kittiwake, fulmar, chough, stonechat and red-legged partridge, although the latter prefer the adjacent fields.

Simply keep going along the coastal path – you don't have a choice – until you meet a kissing-gate at the northern end of **Corrins Hill**, the prominent folly-topped hill that has been in view since near the start of the walk and which stands guardian over the town of Peel. Through the gate, bear right on a grassy track that soon merges with another and bears round to run alongside a wall, heading towards the folly atop Corrins Hill. When the path and wall change direction, do likewise, descending to a ladder/stile giving onto a rough, descending path leading

The parish church is soon reached on the left, and has some interesting stained glass windows depicting scenes from the bible as well as Manx saints.

down to a small row of houses.

At the houses, take the track going left and follow this through numerous twists and turns (all obvious) until, finally, it slips down to meet the Peel–Glen Maye road. Turn right and walk along the road as far as **Kirk Patrick**, and there take the side road for St John's. ◄

Continue past the church for about 300m and then leave the road by turning right onto a greenway (Barnell Lane), setting off initially as a surfaced lane. When the surfacing ends, a rough track continues, climbing steadily throughout its length, flanked by drystone walls and gorse bushes, and offering a fine retrospective view of Peel and Corrins Hill.

Eventually the track emerges onto a surfaced lane. Here turn right and follow the lane, a generally quiet and peaceful prospect, all the way back to Glen Maye. On entering the village, near the former Post Office, bear left down Hillside Terrace to return to the start.

WALK 23

Glen Maye, Niarbyl Bay and Dalby Mountain

Start/Finish	Glen Maye (SC 235 798)
Distance	11km (6¾ miles)
Height gain	392m (1286ft)
Refreshments	Waterfall Country Pub, Glen Maye; café at Niarbyl
Parking	Opposite Waterfall pub

Glen Maye is one of the most beautiful of the Manx National Glens and Niarbyl Bay among the most tranquil and relaxing places on the island. Combining both with a return across the internationally rare habitat of mountain heath that comprises Dalby Mountain brings together three very potent elements that hallmark all that is outstanding about walking on this modestly sized island.

From the car park, go down steps into the top end of the glen and soon cross a bridge above the waterfall. Take the steps descending to the base of the waterfall and then, having viewed it, continue on a riverside path. Lower down the glen, at a path junction, remain with the riverside path to reach the remains of a waterwheel. Here, leave the glen by turning up to a gate, and then head left onto a narrow

track start-
ing down the
narrowing glen, flanked, especially on the right, by high
cliffs on which breeding fulmars can often be seen in the
early summer.

Glen Maye – or Glen Mea, 'the luxuriant glen', as it
was once known – comprises almost 5ha (12 acres),
situated on either side of the Rushen River, and contains a splendid waterfall. In the lower paddock is

In Glen Maye: tranquil and luxurious

the Mona Erin Wheelcase, the only extant evidence of the mining that took place here between 1740 and 1870. Although lead was found, it was generally poor quality and in insufficient quantities to support a major industry. Most of the trees in the glen are sycamore, elm or ash, with some reintroduced oak.

On reaching the bay, where the Rushen River meets the sea, turn sharply up to the left onto a path ascending the headland. This leads to a gate giving into a large pasture; go forward up the right-hand edge to a sign-post sending the path to the right along a sunken path flanked by gorse and wind-blown hawthorn. At the end of the path turn left, up another path. At the top turn right through a kissing-gate and go forward alongside a gorse hedgerow, eventually to arrive at another kissing-gate giving onto an enclosed path leading out to the Dalby–Glen Maye road. Turn right and follow the road to the village of **Dalby**, turning right onto a descending road to Niarbyl.

There is a large café just before the descent to the beach.

◀ On reaching **Niarbyl**, with its attractive thatched cottage, branch left onto a narrow, rising path onto the headland above the bay. With numerous retrospective views of Niarbyl Bay, the path flirts with clifftop edges, wanders down steps to another cove and along its shore, and then starts climbing again, this time on a broader track. Go past a bench (ideally placed for a breather) and keep forward up a flight of steps.

Beach cottage, Niarbyl (featured in the film 'Waking Ned')

Immediately after a fence gap, leave the main path going forward and bear left onto a waymarked path, narrow and climbing. At the top of the climb, turn left over a

96

stile beside a waymark and go forward alongside a fence to a kissing-gate. Through this go forward along a grassy path at the top edge of a field, and walk out to a gate and ladder/stile. Over this, turn right onto an ascending rocky path. Climb to a ladder/stile at a signpost where the Raad ny Foillan branches right below **Creagan Mooar** Brooghs, and here leave the coastal path by bearing left up a stony path ascending through gorse.

Climb to go past a gate, continuing with the track, which is now running parallel with the edge of **Kerroodhoo Plantation** on the left. At the next gate the track finally reaches the plantation edge, which it accompanies to meet a surfaced lane at the top edge of the plantation. Turn left onto the lane and follow it out to meet a road.

At the road junction head left for about 200m and there leave the road by turning right onto a narrow signed path, heading out on the **Dalby Mountain** Nature Reserve. The path is flanked by heather, which in autumn is a delight to see. In the distance, the tower on Corrins Hill above Peel eases into view. ▶

From the road, before reaching the footpath signpost, there is a variant path in the form of a broad rutted track that loops northwards to join the original line, but this is not a right of way, despite regular use by walkers.

The 28.4ha (70-acre) **Dalby Mountain Nature Reserve** comprises traditional heather moorland and is popular with a wide range of bird species including red grouse, hen harrier, curlew, snipe, skylark, meadow pipit and wheatear. Patches of the wet heath are dominated by ling, purple moor grass and rushes, and bog asphodel. Other species include devil's bit scabious, cross-leaved heath and several orchids. The reserve has over 5 per cent of the island's wet heath and is an internationally rare habitat.

Eventually the moorland path descends to a track junction. Here, go forward through a gate and onto a continuing sunken track. The course of the track across the moors is always clear and, beyond the gate, undergoes a number of transformations from wide grassy swards to narrow rocky gullies flowing with water, but always heading in a clear direction. This is a delightfully robust section of the walk and ends at a metal gate giving onto a lane at the edge of **Glen Maye** village. Turn left and follow the lane out to the main valley road. Bear right and follow the road for what is the short distance back to the starting point at the head of Glen Maye.

WALK 24

Glen Maye to Glen Rushen

Start/Finish	Glen Maye car park (SC 235 798)
Distance	10km (6¼ miles)
Height gain	385m (1263ft)
Refreshments	Waterfall Country Pub
Parking	At start

This fine circuit of Dalby Mountain Nature Reserve begins in the village of Glen Maye. When you learn that *maye* is Manx for 'yellow', and see the vast swathes of gorse that cloak the hillsides here, you'll understand where the name came from. But this walk heads away from Glen Maye onto the neighbouring expanse of Dalby Mountain – a significant nature reserve of prime heathland – before turning back towards Glen Maye to pass the old slate quarries of Glen Rushen.

Set off from the car park at Glen Maye and turn right, going down the road in the direction of Dalby and, after about 250m, branch left onto a narrow lane running alongside a stream. Follow this as far as the last property, and there turn right (at a sign 'Unsuitable for Motor Vehicles') onto a sunken track.

The track climbs steadily and is initially narrow and flanked by embankments and hedgerows. Later it narrows even more before reaching level ground above. Farmland predominates for a while before the track finally reaches the edge of the **Dalby Mountain** Nature Reserve at a gate.

Here, go forward along a broad track cutting a line across the heather moorland, eventually to reach a road. Turn left and follow the road alongside the **Glen Rushen Plantation** until finally it reaches the crossroads, near the dome of South Barrule, known as the **Round Table**.

Shortcut via Glen Rushen
About 450m after joining the road from the heathland, it is possible to turn left onto the Bayr ny Skeddan on a signposted route that descends through the Lhargan Plantation and meets up with the main line on the edge of **Glen Rushen**. Taking this option would save about 1.6km (1 mile).

Continue up the road to the so-called Round Table, and turn left at the crossroads. A few strides later branch left through a gate onto a Greenway Road descending towards the Round Table Plantation ahead. Another gate gives into this plantation, through which a clear, rutted path descends to another gate on the far side.

Now go forward into a path enclosed by low walls, passing a derelict croft and steadily

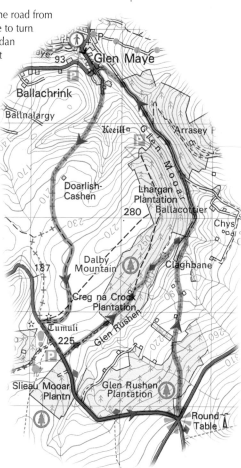

99

following a clear track passing below chimneys and ruined buildings of an industrial past at Beckwith's Vein, one of the principal lead mines on the island. Soon enter Glen Rushen, shortly after linking up once more with the Bayr ny Skeddan. Now the old valley road, no longer used and in places seasonally overgrown, takes the route through Glen Rushen for a little over 800m until a waymarked path descends on the left to run above the River Maye.

The path gradually descends to the riverbank and then crosses it by a footbridge. Over the bridge, bear right through gorse. At a signpost turn left onto a broad track leading out to the lane used at the start of the walk. There turn right and walk out to join the Glen Maye to Dalby road, once more bearing right to walk back up to the Waterfall pub.

LEAD MINING

It is not known when lead mining started in the Isle of Man, though it is certainly the first recorded industry, a mining charter having been granted to the monks of Furness Abbey in 1246 by King Harald Olaffson. The Manx mining industry reached its zenith around the middle of the 19th century, with the main areas being at Laxey and Foxdale. The Foxdale vein runs almost east to west, with the most westerly vein being Beckwith's, above Glen Rushen, and encountered on this walk. The mine was sunk in 1881 following the chance discovery of a lump of galena (lead ore) by a man driving a hay cart. The shaft at Beckwith's descends 335m (1100ft). When you take into account that the mine buildings are only 180m (590ft) above sea level, it follows that the mine shaft descends to 155m (510ft) below sea level.

WALK 25

*Glen Maye, Glen Rushen and the
Postman's Path*

Start/Finish	Glen Maye (SC 236 798)
Distance	1.5km (1 mile), plus 2km (1½ miles) if the walk to the shore is included
Height gain	50m (165ft), plus 85m (280ft) for the shore walk
Refreshments	Waterfall Country Pub
Parking	Opposite the pub

Glen Maye means the 'yellow glen' and a walk through it in spring and early summer amply shows why: gorse bushes cover the glen sides and the farmland above bringing a vivid golden hue to the landscape. The glen came into Manx National Heritage ownership in 1960, and comprises about 11½ acres on either side of the Rushen River: its main feature is a lovely waterfall and lush flora. The Glen's beautiful sheltered fern-filled woodland includes relics of the ancient forest that once covered the island.

The descent into Glen Maye requires little description; it begins from the car park, descending steps into the top end of the woodland. The path is clear and obvious all the way as far as the remains of a waterwheel. ▶

From the waterwheel walk up the nearby road and go left to walk down to the seashore. Retrace your steps to the car park,

The past passes through woodland that is alive in springtime with birdsong and bright with the colour of wild flowers.

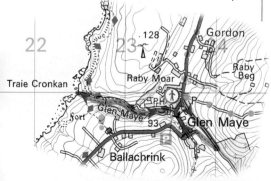

101

and turn left into the village, going up Hillside Terrace and turn right onto a side lane (Glen Rushen Road) that ultimately leads, as its name suggests, through to Glen Rushen. Follow this beyond the last house (Sunridge, on the left), where the road ends. The ongoing glen road is a delight to be followed, but only as far as a signed path descending on the right above the **Glen Maye River**.

The path eases down to the riverbank and then crosses it at a footbridge. Over the bridge bear right through gorse – keep an eye open for grey herons that like to feed in this sheltered spot. At or just before a signpost turn left onto a broad track (the Postman's Path) leading out to a lane (Sound Road). There turn right and walk out to join the Glen Maye to Dalby road, once more bearing right to walk back up to the Waterfall pub.

WALK 26
Cronk ny Arrey Laa

Start/Finish	Parking area at the Sloc (SC 232 748)
Alt Start/Finish	Road bend at SC 217 733
Distance	4.5km (2¾ miles); from the road bend: 1.6km (1 mile)
Height gain	250m (820ft); from the road bend: 80m (263ft)
Parking	Available at both starting points

This summit played an important part in the history of the defence of the island, notably as a watching post during the time of the Vikings – its name means the 'Hill of the Day Watch' – and its conquest today is well worth the effort. If you don't have time for the main route from the Sloc it's only a mile there and back to nip up from the road bend to the east. In spite of the relative ease with which the hill can be gathered in, it sits at the heart of some of the most demanding and spectacular coastal scenery on the island.

Starting from the roadside parking area, cross to the right-hand one of two gates and, through this, turn right onto a rising grassy track passing to the right of a small hillock. You are following the Raad ny Foillan here and the route to the summit trig pillar is very clear throughout; it is a steady pull, but nothing like so difficult an ascent as appears from the roadside.

From the top of the hill the simplest descent is back the way you came, but it is also possible to branch off in an easterly direction on a clear and direct path

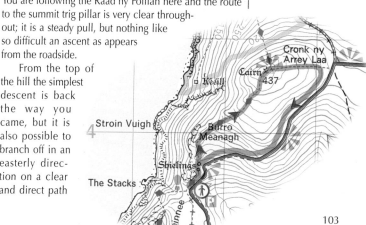

103

(see short way up below) towards a road. Just before reaching the road, turn right and follow an initially stony path, parallel with the road, and later swinging round a shoulder of the hill and leading, occasionally using boardwalks, back down to the Sloc. This descent has the advantage of outstanding viewpoints embracing Port St Mary, Port Erin, the Calf of Man and the long ridge of Lhiattee ny Beinnee.

> The small hillock passed at the start of this section is the site of a **Pictish village**, and looking back from Cronk ny Arrey Laa it is possible to identify the outlines of a group of hut circles. There was also a Neolithic defensive site here, surrounded by wooden palisades and a ditch.

The short way up
From the road bend at SC 217 733, this short and simple ascent is ideal for a short leg-stretch, and begins through a kissing-gate at the head of the rough track leading down to Eary Cushlin. Through the gate, walk beside the wall to join a clear track rising gently to the trig pillar near the summit, and the cairn/mound beyond. Return the same way.

The summit of Cronk ny Arrey Laa, looking toward South Barrule

WALK 27
South Barrule Summit

Start/Finish	Round Table (SC 247 757)
Distance	2km (1¼ miles)
Height gain	170m (558ft)
Parking	At junction of Bayr ny Skeddan and Dalby road (limited)

This brief walk is for those who simply want to 'conquer' South Barrule, one of the principal summits on the island, a Marilyn for those who like to gather such oddities, but most importantly an important prehistoric site with an impressive hill fort.

There is a small amount of roadside parking space where the **Bayr ny Skeddan** emerges from Corlea Plantation and meets the main road near **Round Table**. Here a kissing-gate gives onto a path through heather that climbs unerringly to the summit of South Barrule. It requires no description, and is neither steep nor overlong.

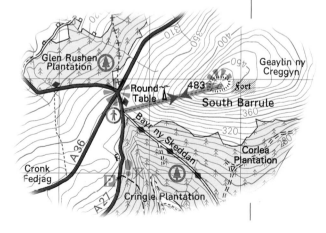

Thoughts that the **Round Table** might have some association with King Arthur and his knights should be instantly dispelled. The origin of the name lies in an insignificant heather-topped mound between the start of this walk and the crossroads nearby. It lies just over the wall on the parish boundary, a small tumulus of significance unknown, but, being called the 'Round Table' is said to be the place where the watchers on the summit would gather to take their meals – an unlikely story, of course.

A fine Celtic Iron Age hill fort encloses the summit of **South Barrule**, at 483m (1585ft) the main defensive stronghold in the south of the island in prehistoric times, and the highest and largest hill fort on the island. The original inner rampart was largely destroyed, but encloses the remains of many circular huts. The fort was later enlarged by the construction of massive outer stone ramparts, and partially excavated during 1960–1961 and 1968. It bears many similarities with pre-Roman tribal hill forts found in southern Britain.

The shapely summit of South Barrule

It is a fine vantage point and takes in most of the southern part of the island, a distinction that made it one of the 'early warning' Watch Hills, part of a defensive line of hills along the western coast during the Norse occupation of the island.

From the summit, simply go back by the line of ascent. ▸

Walk 28 describes an extended walk across the summit and down the other side.

WALK 28

South Barrule Forest Walk and Corlea Plantation

Start/Finish	South Barrule Plantation (SC 275 767)
Distance	8.5km (5¼ miles)
Height gain	315m (1033ft)
Parking	At start

I may be alone in this, but I experience a peculiar sense of privilege when I find myself in the middle of some prehistoric settlement, like the Iron Age hill fort encountered on the highest point of this walk. It's the notion that prehistoric man may well have perched on the same rock as me, eating the Iron Age equivalent of a pork pie and pickled egg and almost certainly gazing out across a landscape that, apart from the absence of trees and the presence of radio masts on Snaefell, would not have been noticeably different from the view you see today.

There is a fair amount of free range wandering on this walk, through acres of heather: none of it is especially difficult, except after prolonged rain. But if all you want is to tick off another Marilyn then refer to Walk 27; this walk is for those who like to wander 'lonely as a cloud'.

Begin from the car park at the entrance to the South Barrule Forest Park on the Foxdale side of the hill. Go past the car park, through a gate/stile and then forward along the left-hand one of two broad tracks running into **South Barrule Plantation**. This track roughly parallels the Castletown road and, ignoring branching trails, in due course emerges

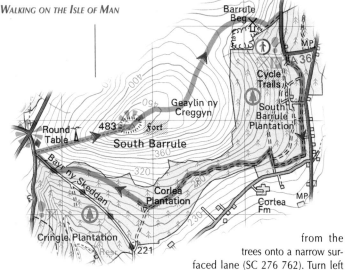

from the trees onto a narrow surfaced lane (SC 276 762). Turn left for a few strides, and then, just before reaching the road, bear right onto a continuing plantation trail.

Ignore any branching tracks and access points, but continue always just within the forest boundary, even when it changes direction. In due course, the track comes to an obvious junction. Left is a way out of the plantation to a road (SC 273 754); right, the track climbs gently into the plantation. Turn right, uphill, but only for about 200m (ignore branching trails, left and right), and then go left along a descending track that quite soon emerges into a more open area, with fine views south to Derby Haven and Langness.

A short way on, press on into the Corlea Plantation, where the ongoing track is a delight to follow. ◄

When the track forks at a distinct junction (SC 259 751), branch right. A little distance further on, at another meeting of tracks, keep forward onto a track/path that leads through a wide firebreak, more or less contouring across the southern slopes of South Barrule.

The path through the firebreak eventually climbs gently to run along the top boundary of the plantation, and leads to a fence corner, beyond which lies a rough

Because the plantation is more open, it is easier to see a wider range of birdlife, with stonechat, wheatear, warblers and the occasional visiting hen harrier putting in an appearance.

partially surfaced lane used by the **Bayr ny Skeddan**. Turn right onto this and, just before reaching a surfaced road, leave the lane at a kissing-gate for a clear path striking up the south-west ridge of **South Barrule**. The angle is not as daunting as it seems end on, and a brisk walk will bring you to the summit in less than half an hour.

On the slopes of South Barrule

A fine Celtic Iron Age hill fort encloses the **summit of South Barrule**, at 483m (1585ft) the main defensive stronghold in the south of the island in prehistoric times, and the highest and largest hill fort on the island. The original inner rampart was largely destroyed, but encloses the remains of many circular huts. The fort was later enlarged by the construction of massive outer stone ramparts, and partially excavated during 1960–1961 and 1968. It bears many similarities to pre-Roman tribal hill forts found in southern Britain.

From the summit continue roughly in the same direction as on the ascent for a while. A path of sorts begins the descent through heather, on the way passing through the hill fort outer defences. Continue to a large boulder, where the now-narrow path divides. Here branch left: soon the path runs blind, leaving walkers to figure out the easiest way on. The blanket heather is short and there are numerous sheep tracks as well as the occasional vehicle track to ease progress. Initially, a useful target is the masted summit of Snaefell in the far distance, or the Kionslieu Reservoir, rather nearer and visible to the right of Barrule Beg, the subsidiary top of South Barrule.

Before long, the top of the **South Barrule Plantation** comes into view, with a quarry to its left. This, too, is a useful target, but aim well to the left (north) of the quarry: a rough bearing on Barrule Beg is the best way down.

Eventually, at a fence (before crossing onto **Barrule Beg**), follow this to the right to a fence corner just above the quarry. Here an old gate continues the route downhill alongside the top edge of the quarry (fence). When the fence changes direction, keep on for a little while longer, but gradually work down through deeper heather to a cluster of sheep pens close by the quarry access track.

At the sheep pens find a way to a wooden gate giving onto a vehicle track that leads down to the quarry access and then out to the road. Turn right, walking downhill to return to the car park at the start of the walk.

WALK 29

Lhiattee ny Beinnee and Fleshwick Bay

Start/Finish	The Sloc road bend (SC 217 733)
Distance	8.4km (5¼ miles)
Height gain	457m (1500ft)
Parking	At start

This is a stunning walk every step of the way. The initial climb to the top of Lhiattee ny Beinnee is nothing like so daunting as it appears from the roadside and, once on top of the ridge, the walking is delightfully easy. The views, initially northwards towards Niarbyl Bay, are impressive and improve once the route descends to bring Fleshwick Bay in on the act. By a roundabout route, the walk returns across the heather moorland of Lhiattee ny Beinnee's eastern flanks.

Begin from the parking space at the roadside and cross to the left-hand one of two gates opposite, which gives access to one of the island's Greenway Roads, Bayr Glass, along which this walk will conclude. Through the gate go forward on a narrow path through heather leading to the steep northern slopes of **Lhiattee ny Beinnee**. Follow a clear path, climbing steadily and with ever-improving views northwards to Niarbyl Bay, ultimately to reach the large cairn of quartz boulders that marks the summit of this elongated mountain ridge. ▶

The ongoing track traverses the summit ridge and then starts to descend as Port Erin, Port St Mary and the steep-sided defile of Fleshwick Bay come into view. Dropping more steeply, the path descends eventually to a wall corner and ladder/stile. Over the stile, continue descending to a signpost and then going down alongside a low wall at the head of **Fleshwick Bay**.

In late summer the ridge is a particular delight, a canvas of heather purple and gorse yellow highlighted by random tufts of cotton grass.

111

Fleshwick Bay, a popular and secluded spot

The path finally reaches the edge of Fleshwick Bay where it meets a lane. The bay itself is sheltered and a popular place with divers, the waters are clear and the setting ideal for lazing away the day.

Turn left, following the lane for a few hundred metres, as far as a signed path on the right. Leave the lane here and walk up to the lower edge of Fleshwick Plantation. Turn left along the

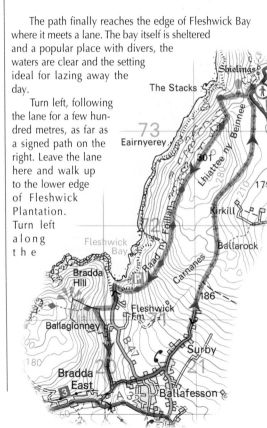

foot of the plantation on a broad green track between drystone walls. Shortly, the path merges with a farm access track. Continue in the same direction, walking out through a gorse-studded landscape. Keep going as far as the first building on the left, just beyond which a signed path branches sharply left.

Turn here and soon enter a rising pathway flanked by gorse that climbs to a surfaced lane. Keep ahead along this to meet a road and again go forward, continuing to a T-junction. Turn left (signposted 'Surby only') onto an ascending lane.

At the top of the lane, maintain the same direction, now on a bridleway leading to a gate giving onto the Bayr Glass. Through the gate, strike out across open heathland, climbing steadily but not excessively so. The track follows a delightful course across the eastern slopes of **Lhiattee ny Beinnee**, with superb forward views of Cronk ny Arrey Laa, and across the island to the distant settlement of Castletown. Continue following the moorland track to return to the starting point.

WALK 30

Bradda Head and Bradda Hill

Start/Finish	Bradda Glen car park (SC 192 697)
Distance	5.5km (3½ miles)
Height gain	280m (920ft)
Refreshments	Pubs and cafés in Port Erin
Parking	At start

The ascent from sea level to the top of Bradda Hill can seem much more than it is on a hot day. But as a rule there's a sea breeze blowing and this helps enormously. The view from Bradda Head, the first key point reached, is outstanding and extends to the mountains of Northern Ireland as well as the coast of southern Scotland. The onward route continues to Bradda Hill itself; for those who collect such summits, this is one of the island's Marilyns.

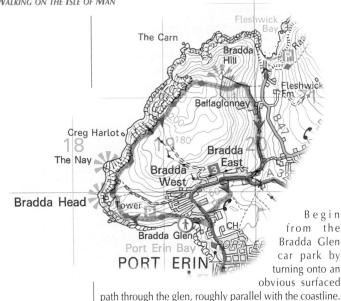

The Carn

Fleshwick Bay

Bradda Hill

Fleshwick

Ballaglonney

Creg Harlot

18   19   180

The Nay

Bradda East

Bradda West   3

Bradda Head

Tower

Bradda Glen

Port Erin Bay

PORT ERIN

Bradda Glen

Begin from the Bradda Glen car park by turning onto an obvious surfaced path through the glen, roughly parallel with the coastline. Follow this, with ever improving views until it divides:

114

either way will do, but the right branch leads briefly up to a wooden gate giving onto a broad green track that leads to a kissing-gate (on the left) from where a broad track climbs steadily towards **Milner Tower**. Halfway up the ascending, grassy track a path leaves left and makes a direct ascent to the tower. Easier going is found by sticking to the track to arrive at level ground north-east of the tower, from which it is simple enough to backtrack to take in the view that the tower offers.

WILLIAM MILNER

The monument on the top of Bradda Head is dedicated to William Milner in grateful acknowledgement of his many charities to the poor of Port Erin, and for his never tiring efforts for the benefit of the Manx fishermen. Milner, from

Milner Tower, erected by public subscription

Liverpool, was a safe maker by profession. He was instrumental in securing the erection of the breakwater at Port Erin. The tower was erected by public subscription in 1871, and when the foundation stone was laid, Milner threw a huge party to which, it seems, the whole neighbourhood was invited. The tower was completed during his lifetime and is said to be fashioned after one of his keys.

Affixed to Milner Tower is a plaque announcing that a short distance away the winner of the Kodak 'World's Best Photograph' competition was taken! Today, you might gaze out over sea cliffs and wonder what was so special. But the photographer, CW Powell of Manchester, took a photograph of his fiancée in the sunset and won prize money of £4000.

From the tower a clear track descends to a nearby signpost from which an ongoing path continues up the slopes of Bradda Hill: for those not of a nervous disposition, a narrow track hugs the top edge of the sea cliffs and provides some spectacular views of the sea cliffs.

Eventually the path leads to less intimidating ground, but continues to parallel the cliffs, now climbing steadily as it mounts the heather shoulder of Bradda Hill. At first the path courts an old fenceline (on the left) but, at a wall corner and stile, switches sides and then follows a wall almost to the summit of the hill.

A brief diversion is now needed to reach the summit cairn on **Bradda Hill**, one of only five Marilyns on the island, such being a hill that is at least 500ft (roughly 150m) higher than the land around it.

From the top of Bradda Hill take the obvious path heading down towards unseen Fleshwick Bay. It drops steeply to a wall gap with good views northwards to Niarbyl Bay, and then continues, still descending through heather, to reach the bottom edge of Fleshwick Plantation. There turn right along a broad green track enclosed by walls.

Soon the track merges with a farm access track, which later runs on to meet the end of a surfaced lane (Ernie Broadbent Walk), and trots out to meet a road. Turn right into **Bradda East**, walking for about 200m, to a sign-posted path on the left, passing along a building gable onto an enclosed path along the edge of an arable field. Cross a stone step/stile and walk down the right-hand edge of a field.

Lower down the field another stile gives onto the edge of a golf course. Walk forward for a short distance, and then, when you reach a the corner of a wall, turn right, following the edge of the golf course (taking care to evade miss-hit golf balls – or, better, make sure that those who might hit them know you are there!) until, on the far side of the course, you can dip to the right along a narrow footpath to emerge at a road near a **telephone box**.

Turn left and shortly turn in through the arched entrance to **Bradda Glen** and walk on to return to the start.

WALK 31

Port Erin to Peel

Start	Port Erin railway station (SC 197 689)
Finish	Fenella Beach, Peel (SC 241 843)
Distance	22.7km (14 miles)
Height gain	1250m (4100ft)
Refreshments	Pubs and cafés in Port Erin, Various cafés and pubs in Peel

This is an outstanding walk which, taken in full, demands a good deal of stamina as it involves three significant ascents, two from sea level. In terms of height gain, it equates with climbing Ben Nevis; in distance it is greater than that. So expect a long and energetic day. For much, but not all, of the way the walk follows the line of the Raad ny Foillan, on one of its more demanding days.

The coastal scenery throughout is of the highest order, the birdlife is diverse, the wild flowers likewise, and the walk a long succession of pleasures that make turning round and walking back the next day a tempting proposition. Failing that, you'll need to organise transport either to take you to the start or pick you up as a rather steamy roadside bundle near Peel Castle. Public transport, of course, serves both towns extremely well.

The walk begins by tackling Bradda Head and the subsequent and higher Bradda Hill. From there a lovely descent sweeps down to Fleshwick Bay before engaging low gear for the pull onto Lhiattee ny Beinnee. Another plunging descent brings you out to the road at the Sloc before romping to the high point of the walk, Cronk ny Arrey Laa. From here you next head down to sea level at Niarbyl from where an easy walk leads to the mouth of Glen Maye. But even there you haven't finished, for more coastal walking leads north to Corrins Hill beyond which lie Peel Castle and the end of the day.

Leave Port Erin by walking towards the seafront, and there turn right to walk up the main road in the direction of the conspicuous tower on **Bradda Head**. Quit the road at the arched entrance to Bradda Glen and soon go past the glen

117

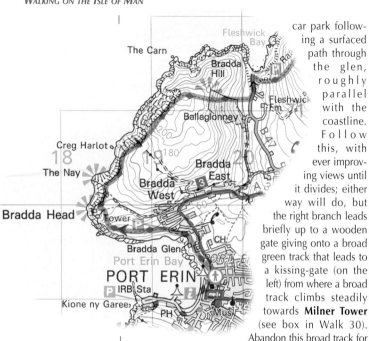

car park following a surfaced path through the glen, roughly parallel with the coastline. Follow this, with ever improving views until it divides; either way will do, but the right branch leads briefly up to a wooden gate giving onto a broad green track that leads to a kissing-gate (on the left) from where a broad track climbs steadily towards **Milner Tower** (see box in Walk 30). Abandon this broad track for a narrow, steep path on the left, to visit the tower itself.

From the tower, a clear track descends to a nearby signpost from which a broad path continues up onto Bradda Hill, but, for those not of a nervous disposition, a narrow track hugs the top edge of the sea cliffs and provides some spectacular views, not only of the cliffs, but of the numerous sea birds that frequent them. Eventually the path leads to less intimidating ground, but continues to parallel the sea cliffs, now climbing steadily as it mounts the heather shoulder of Bradda Hill. At first the path courts an old fenceline (on the left) but, at a wall corner and stile, switches sides and then follows a wall almost to the summit of the hill. A brief diversion is needed to reach the summit cairn on **Bradda Hill**, one of only five Marilyns on the island, such being a hill that is at least 500ft (roughly 150m) higher than the land around it.

Bradda Head from the edge of Port Erin bay

From the top of Bradda Hill take the obvious path heading down towards unseen Fleshwick Bay. It drops quite steeply to a wall gap, with good views northwards to Niarbyl Bay, and then continues, still descending through heather, to reach the bottom edge of Fleshwick Plantation.

map continues on page 120

Go forward, descending along a field edge to a narrow lane leading, left, down to **Fleshwick Bay**, but just before reaching the bay, step right over a small stream and begin quite a steep climb, initially alongside a fence, but then linking footpath signposts along a clear path that swings about to take the sting out of the ascent. If in doubt, keep going up, and this dubious technique – although adequate here – will eventually intercept a broad and clear track across the top of the mountain, **Lhiattee ny Beinnee**, an elongated ridge topped by a cairn of large quartz boulders.

map continues on page 121

Continue in the same direction and gradually come onto a descending stretch, with lovely coastal views. The path drops steadily through heather and reaches another road at a conspicuous bend; this is The Sloc. Go through the road gate and then immediately left through another beside it. Then turn right, passing around a small hillock to begin the long pull up onto **Cronk ny Arrey Laa**. The route is very direct and very clear, leading unerringly to a huge cairn on the summit of the hill. This summit can be avoided by staying along a new-ish path from the Sloc gate, and which rises parallel with the road, and then rounds a shoulder of the hill to continue easily to join the prominent track coming down from the summit.

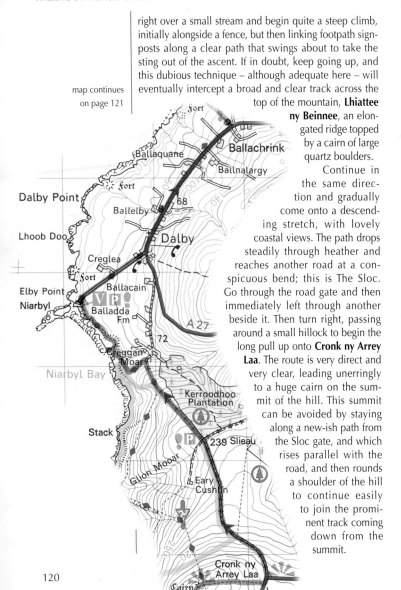

120

Although there is little to see on the ground, the small hillock passed at the start of this section is the site of a **Pictish village**, and the site was also once occupied by Neolithic farmers who built a defensive stronghold on the hill, surrounded by a wooden palisade and a ditch. The outline of the dwellings can be seen from the slopes of Cronk ny Arrey Laa.

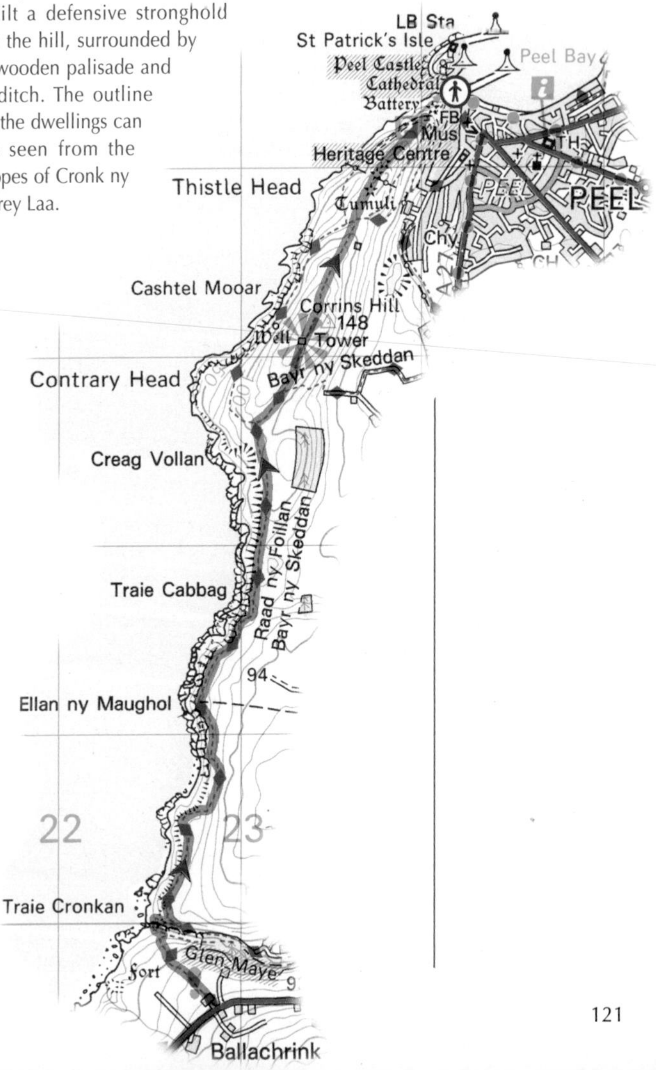

LB Sta
St Patrick's Isle
Peel Castle
Cathedral
Battery
Peel Bay
Mus
Heritage Centre
Thistle Head
Tumuli
Chy
PEEL
Cashtel Mooar
Corrins Hill
148
Tower
Well
Bayr ny Skeddan
Contrary Head
Creag Vollan
Raad ny Foillan
Bayr ny Skeddan
Traie Cabbag
94
Ellan ny Maughol
22
23
Traie Cronkan
Glen Maye
Fort
9
Ballachrink

121

The **summit** of Cronk ny Arrey Laa is a prehistoric burial mound dating from the early Bronze Age. It was excavated in 1958. The summit is known as a Watch Hill, part of a defensive line of hills along the western coast of the island. From the top of the hill there is a spectacular view of most of the southern part of the island, so being a watchman was a responsible position with harsh penalties for failure to be on duty or for sleeping while on duty: these ranged from forfeiting *bodye* and *goodes*, to a *cowe* and *lyfe* and *lyme*.

Thus far the walk has followed the coastal path, the Raad ny Foillan ('the Way of the Gulls'), but for a while it leaves this by turning east from the top of Cronk ny Arrey Laa, passing the trig pillar and heading down a

Looking back to Bradda Hill from Niarbyl

122

clear and broad track towards the road. Turn left just before exiting onto the road, and follow a wallside path to a kissing-gate giving onto a broad, walled track. Go left, down this; it descends around Eary Cushlin to a track junction at the edge of Kerroodhoo Plantation. Keep forward, initially alongside the plantation, then moving slightly away from it, but eventually descending a stony gully to reach houses at a road end. Here, turn left to follow a waymarked route around field edges that eventually descends to arguably the most beautiful spot on the whole island, Niarbyl Bay.

Delightful every step of the way, the path teases a route around sea cliffs and drops to a stony bay, used as a film location for the 'Irish-set' film 'Waking Ned'. Continue with the obvious path and soon reach the charming niche at Niarbyl where 'Ned Devine's' thatched cottage sits beside an ancient cannon.

A bit of road walking now ensues. Turn up the road serving Niarbyl and walk up to Dalby. Manx National Heritage has opened a café at Niarbyl, and this would be a convenient point to take a break. From there, continue up the road to a T-junction. Turn left along the Dalby road and follow this for about 1.6km (1 mile), now once more on the Raad ny Foillan. At Cronkmoar, the path leaves the road at the side of a house and pursues a signed route down to the mouth of Glen Maye – the yellow glen. Why yellow? Visit in summer and see for yourself: gorse, everywhere, and beautiful it is, too.

On reaching Glen Maye it is possible to cross the in-flowing stream and make a steep and direct assault on the headland on the other side. But it is easier if longer to turn right and walk up the glen to the signed coastal path, now also part of the Bayr ny Skeddan, and there turning left onto a rising path.

The path climbs briefly and, not far above the bay, branches. Bear right as the path then adopts a superb line across the top of cliffs and headlands, constantly undulating and changing direction in a way that makes the walk invigorating and encouraging. This is where binoculars come into their own. ▶

A wide range of birds can be seen on the cliffs, from herring gulls to kittiwakes and fulmars. Choughs and stonechats are also a common sight and partridges are no strangers to the adjacent fields.

Simply keep going along the coastal path – you don't have a choice – until you meet a kissing-gate at the northern end of Corrins Hill, the prominent folly-topped hill that has been in view since near the start of the walk and which stands guardian over the town of Peel. Through the gate, bear right on a grassy track that soon merges with another and bears round to run alongside a wall, heading towards the folly. As the wall turns abruptly to the right, leave it by going forward onto Corrins Hill.

Cross the hill and begin an easy descent towards Peel Castle. A number of routes now come and go, but it is not difficult to figure out the easiest way down, a route that emerges at a car park at Fenella Beach, one of the smallest beaches on the island. Peel Castle stands nearby, and marks the end of the walk, but is well worth a visit, providing, as it does, a relaxing end to the day.

WALK 32
Mull Hill, Spanish Head and The Chasms

Start/Finish	Port Erin (SC 195 690)
Distance	8.5km (5¼ miles)
Height gain	303m (994ft)
Refreshments	Port Erin, Cregneash (seasonal)
Parking	Port Erin

I had long looked at the tangle of footpaths that radiate from Cregneash with a view to sorting out a walk across the middle of this southern bit of the island, but always been distracted by the stunning coastal route between Port St Mary and Port Erin. As my weeks on the island came to a close, I finally succumbed, on the very last day, foregoing a moorland tramp north of Baldwin for the pathways of Rushen: and I was mightily glad that I did, because it turned out to be superb even though it had parts in common with other walks.

Begin from the sea front in Port Erin and walk towards the Bay Hotel, immediately beyond which a surfaced pathway on the left rises to reach a large house converted to apartments. Walk round this and turn up the access driveway to meet a rough lane fronting more houses (**Darrag**). ▶

Turn left and walk out to a surfaced lane, meeting it at a bend. Turn right, ascending, and, taking great care against approaching traffic, keep going until the gradient eases and you reach a largish grassy lay-by on the left-hand side of the road. Up above is a distinct, fenced area. Take the footpath that leads up to this and, over a step/stile, enter the grounds of the Meayll Stone Circle.

Go across another stile at the back, and walk onto the top of **Mull Hill**, site of a

From this point there is a lovely retrospective view over Port Erin to Bradda Hill and Lhiattee ny Beinnee.

Above The Chasms, near Spanish Head

Second World War radar station. Continue through this to locate a prominent and descending broad gravel track that curves back down to the single track road. Turn left onto the road and left again to head for **Cregneash village**. When a branching lane into the village appears, go down this, and keep forward to reach the last thatched cottage on the right (Harry Kelly's Cottage). Turn right here to locate the start of the Church Farm Walk.

> The fields close to **Cregneash village** are now being farmed with methods used in the area from about 1890. Clydesdale horses provide the main motive power. Oats, barley, potatoes, swedes and vegetables like cabbages and carrots can be seen growing together with flax for linen and fibre. Because straw is needed for thatching, wheat is grown although it is not traditional in this area. Most of the holdings in the village were crofts of between 6 and 8 acres (roughly 2–4ha), each supporting two or three cows and some poultry.

Go left, along a walled track, and follow this until the track forks at Spanish Head Road. Here, keep forward, branching left at a signpost. The track twists and turns, flanked by overgrown walls and gorse, and the route is waymarked when it needs to be.

The path finally descends to intercept the coastal path. Go left along it, heading for **The Chasms**, and climbing steadily to an isolated building that was once a café, and still bears the name on one of the gables. Just past it, bear right (signpost) and walk down beside a wall to a step/stile across which you can get a good view of Sugar Loaf and the cliffs of The Chasms. But the route does not cross the stile. Instead, from it, bear left down to a gate and stone stile and, over this, head down to a signpost at the end of a walled lane heading for Port St Mary.

Enter the walled lane, and keep going until in due course it becomes surfaced as the first houses are reached. A short way on, where the lane forks, branch left for The Howe and Port Erin, into Glen Chass.

Continue through Glen Chass and, on the far side, meet the Cregneash road. Turn left, up the road, for about 150m, to a signpost on the right (take the first of two) and here leave the road for a track passing to the left of a barn. When the track reaches a derelict cottage, go ahead over a stile onto a path that leads across fields to emerge near a white cottage at a stile.

Turn onto a signed track, past the cottage and maintaining height across the hillside, heading for a signpost and stile in a wall corner near three gates. Cross the stile and, in the ensuing field, shortly bear left through gorse to another stone stile. Over this, go forward alongside a fence to another stile beside a gate and pass through a nearby kissing-gate onto a wallside path, targeting the tower on Bradda Head. Soon the route reaches a small group of stiles and footpath signposts. Here, over the last of these, beside a metal gate, bear right, down a grassy track between hedgerows.

Continue down to meet a road. Cross this and go forward on a surfaced pathway leading into an estate road. Keep forward to another pathway to the right of a house opposite. This leads into a cul-de-sac. Bear left along another path to pass more houses and walk out to a road junction. Turn left to another junction nearby, and go forward into Athol Park. At the far end of Athol Park, swing right to a main road junction and there turn left to go down to the seafront.

WALK 33
Mull Hill and Cregneash

Start/Finish	Cregneash village car park (SC 191 675)
Distance	2.5km (1½ miles)
Height gain	70m (230ft)
Refreshments	Café in Cregneash village in Chreg-y-Shee cottage
Parking	At start

This brief walk is an introduction to a fascinating corner of the Isle of Man, the Meayll Peninsula, where the heritage village of Cregneash re-creates past times in Man, while the prehistoric remains on Mull (Meayll) Hill tell of even earlier times. The view from the top of Mull Hill is extensive, embracing the whole of the southern part of the island and the Calf of Man. Further away, the Isle of Anglesey and the mountains of North Wales can be seen, as well as those of Northern Ireland and southern Scotland.

Begin from the Cregneash village car park in the old quarry above the village and turn right along the road. Follow the road as it swings to the right, and walk a short distance further, and then branch to the right onto a single track lane flanked by gorse bushes. Follow this lane as far as a wide, grassy lay-by on the right hand side; ignore an earlier and tempting vehicle track rising onto the hill. Up above, is a distinct, fenced area. Take the footpath up to this and, over a step/stile, enter the grounds of the **Meayll Hill** stone circle.

The **'Circle of Stones'** is a series of tombs now dated to 3500bce, the Middle Neolithic age. It was excavated originally in 1893, when cremated human bones, pottery, jet and flints were found. Further excavations produced

The Meayll Hill stone circle

numerous urns with ashes and charcoal, knives and pebbles.

The circle is elliptical and consists of six structures (called tritaphs), which were used as burial chambers. Modern research suggests that cremation would have taken place away from the site and the ashes placed in urns before being carried ceremonially for interment here.

After exploring the area go across another stile at the back, and walk onto the top of **Mull Hill**, site of a Second World War radar station. Continue through this to locate a prominent and broad gravel track that curves back down to the single track lane. Turn left, and then left again towards the village, taking a branching lane on the right down into the centre of **Cregneash**.

The village today is a **living museum** owned by Manx National Heritage, and while it is possible to wander freely along the roads, it is only on payment at the entrance (at Cummel Beg cottage) that you can enter the buildings and learn about life here. The adjacent café is an excellent place at which to enjoy a short break.

CREGNEASH

The tiny village of Cregneash is isolated from the rest of Man, and was the last stronghold of the traditional skills and customs that characterised the crofting way of life. A small community of hardy people prospered here from the middle of the 17th century, combining small-scale farming and other diverse occupations. During the fishing seasons, men here would leave the fields for the trials of the Scottish and Irish waters.

At Cregneash today, the evidence of this rugged lifestyle is re-created, and features Harry Kelly's Cottage, opened in 1938, and portraying today the way of life on the island 150 years ago. Parts of the village featured in the film *Waking Ned*. It is not so long since all the buildings here were thatched, but now only a few remain so.

For many years the people of Cregneash did not have a church. This perturbed the Vicar of Rushen because the people of Cregneash had to walk to his church in all weathers. So he began holding a service one night a week in one of the village houses. By the mid-1870s, the new Vicar encouraged the people of Cregneash to build a church of their own, which they did: everyone gave their labour free, with the result that the church's only expense was for materials (about £150). The church was dedicated to St Peter by the Bishop of Sodor and Man on 13th December 1878, but only the sanctuary was consecrated so that the rest of the building could be used as a school.

Having visited Cregneash simply take the rising road to the right of Cummel Beg, and soon bear right on a rising grassy track that leads up to the main road, not far from the car park.

WALK 34
Port St Mary, The Sound and Port Erin

Start	Port St Mary (SC 211 672)
Finish	Port Erin railway station (SC 197 690)
Alt Finish	Port St Mary (SC 211 672)
Distance	10.5km (6½ miles); or 13.3km (8¼ miles)
Height gain	492m (1614ft)
Refreshments	Port St Mary, The Sound (café), Port Erin
Parking	Car park area along coast, near Kallow Point
Note	Between The Sound and Port Erin, dogs are prohibited, even on leads

This is one of the most pleasing walks in the book, following a section of the Raad ny Foillan (the coastal path) that is constantly changing direction and presenting new views, new panoramas and fresh cliffscapes.

The walk can be organised as a circular route by linking Port Erin and Port St Mary. The options are to walk back from Port Erin railway station to the coastal car park you started from (an additional distance of 2.8km/1¾ miles); take a taxi; or take the short ride on the steam railway to Port St Mary Station and walk back to the car park from there (¾ mile).

From the parking area walk away from Port St Mary until, after the last houses, you can go forward onto a lane (Clifton Road) feeding into the edge of the golf course. Almost immediately keep left onto a path alongside a concrete wall, leading up to an estate road. Turn left, following the road, and shortly head into an estate through which the route is waymarked, and leads to an enclosed path cutting through to another road. Once more, turn left and keep following the road, which skims along above **Perwick Bay**.

On reaching a track junction, maintain the same direction, going over a high ladder/

stile beside a metal gate and continuing ahead on a rough track across a pasture to another ladder/stile. Stick with the ongoing track, which slices through a patchwork of walled fields, at the end of which, emerging from an enclosed section, turn right up a grassy footpath to a wooden gate, and then bear left towards a signpost and stile in a fence on the skyline to the left.

Formed by earth movement, **The Chasms** are a spectacular sight, terminating in the sea far below. Tradition holds that the cracks appeared when Jesus was crucified and the earth quaked. The whole

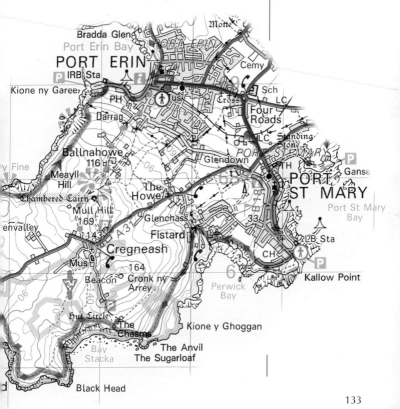

headland is a mass of stunning cliffs in confusion and disarray; indeed the point Kione-y-ghoggan's name means 'headland of disorder'. Inevitably, The Chasms have attracted many stories. Here, for example, the Irish warriors who had assassinated King Olaf I in 1153 were captured by the Manx people and beheaded, their bodies flung into one of the chasms and soil tipped down on top of them, hence the name Skort Sidroryn, 'the chasm of the soldiers'. Further on, another chasm is known as Skort Tashtey, 'the chasm of the treasure', an allusion to the belief than when the Countess of Derby was forced to quit the island in 1651, her treasure was hidden in the chasm. The story adds that the treasure has never been found.

Do not cross the stile (which simply gives access to a viewing point for The Chasms), but instead turn right, walking uphill alongside a wall and then walk up towards what looks like a derelict house but which was the old Chasms café and is today a shelter.

From the shelter, walk parallel with a wall to a large stile with handrails, giving onto a path that heads for the

The sea cliffs of Spanish Head

great expanse of **Spanish Head**, across which a clear footpath cuts through the heather and dwarf gorse. Ignore all branching footpaths and stick to the coastal path (left at a signpost) which clings to the top edge of the cliffs but later moves inland a little as it cuts across to the cliffs of Spanish Head.

An easy wander across the headlands soon brings the Calf of Man into view, with a clear path continuing through heather and gorse, now descending all the while.

The path eventually drops to cross a small footbridge spanning a burn. Go over a step/stile, beyond which a grassy path crosses a low headland before bending around a small cove, Carrick Nay. The ongoing path soon reaches a memorial and wanders across to the café at The Sound.

The Sound is a good place to take a break and it is not unusual to sit among the rocks here and watch a dozen or more grey seals bobbing in the choppy waters of the Little Sound keeping an eye on passers-by.

The **Thousla Cross**, named after the tidal Thousla Rock just offshore, commemorates an act of heroism by men of Rushen parish in their rescue of the crew of the French schooner Jeane St Charles in 1858. The ship was en route to Londonderry in Northern Ireland from Pontrieux, part of a trade that had flourished following the Crimean War, when it got into difficulties and was forced to drop anchor in the channel that separates the Isle of Man from the Calf of Man.

Just beyond the café stands the Thousla Cross, from which walk up to a ladder/stile. Beyond, the path steadily climbs around a headland, becoming narrower and more rocky as it passes **Clett Aldrick** (just marked as Aldrick on the OS 1:50,000 map). It climbs to a stile from which the ongoing path undulates alongside a clifftop fence above **Bay Fine** and through rock outcrops, heather and gorse. ▶ The walking is easy and delightful, everything that clifftop walking should be.

Keep an eye open in springtime and early summer for the delicate pale blue-leaved squill, which grows profusely around here.

Rock fall architecture, above Bay Fine

Gradually, as Port Erin comes into view, the path starts to descend, eventually going down to a wooden kissing-gate at the end of a fence. Continue descending alongside a fence until it changes direction and becomes enclosed between a fence and drystone wall. This in turn leads to a gate beyond which the path descends towards the lifeboat station, there to meet a road. Turn right and walk into **Port Erin**.

The **railway station** is in the main street, at right angles to the beach. Trains operate between the middle of April and late October, and the current timetable is available from all tourist information offices.

Alternative finish in Port St Mary
The shorter option is to take the train to Port St Mary station (taking about five minutes) and then, on arrival, simply turn right out of the station and follow the main road into town, maintaining roughly the same direction throughout finally to emerge at the southern edge of the bay.

To walk all the way back to Port St Mary, continue past Port Erin railway station, and keep going as far as a roundabout. There turn right, now following a road which leads ultimately to the centre of Port St Mary. Maintain the same direction through the town and out the other side to join a road leading out to the coast. Turn right to return to the starting point.

WALK 35

Colby Glen, Ballakilpheric and Bay ny Carrickey

Start/Finish	Bay ny Carrickey (SC 239 686)
Distance	8.7km (5½ miles)
Height gain	145m (475ft)
Refreshments	Pubs at Colby and 1km (½ mile) west of start
Parking	Roadside parking area at junction with Poyllvaaish road

The attractive Colby Glen is just north of the village and centres on Colby River, a delightful burn flowing through a narrow, wooded gorge, which in springtime boasts lovely displays of bluebells and primroses. This walk passes Colby Station, an ideal start for anyone using the steam railway as a means of getting about.

From the parking area, walk westwards towards Port St Mary, as far as another roadside pull-off on the left (SC 234 687) and there cross the road, and go through two gates opposite to follow a field-edge vehicle track. On the far side of the field, go forward through another gate and along the edge of the next field.

The field edge path leads up to the steam railway crossing at **Colby Station**. Over this, go forward through a small housing estate to a crossroads. Cross into Colby Glen Road opposite, noting the interesting village clock on the left. The village name probably derives from the Scandinavian language: *col* meaning hill, and *by* or *byr* indicating a farmstead.

In Colby Glen

Taking care against approaching traffic in the absence of footpaths, continue up the road as far as the gated turning into **Colby Glen** (SC 231 706).

> **Colby Glen** is one of the 17 Manx glens, a place dominated by ash, beech, elm, and sycamore trees: it covers an area of 2.0 hectares or 4.9 acres. This is a truly tranquil place, verdant and filled with birdsong, a setting wherein you could be miles from anywhere.

Go down steps to the river, cross the bridge onto a rising path along the top edge of the glen. Eventually, the path descends to pass a closed bridge at a fern-filled gorge. Press on through delightful woodland to the third bridge (signpost) and there turn left to go up steps onto a narrow footpath leading into a hedgerowed path. Keep on to a kissing-gate, and through it turn right along another hedged path that later opens out onto a broader farm track. Keep forward to a gate at a track junction. Turn left towards **Cronkedooney**, where the track joins a rough-surfaced lane and leads on to a lane corner.

Here, at a signpost, turn left and walk out to another junction opposite **Ballakilpheric Methodist chapel**. Go left and immediately right, shortly passing Ballakilpheric Farm and, further on, the turning into Burn Brae, a large and conspicuous white house on the left. ▸

About 60m later, leave the lane at a signpost by turning left through a kissing-gate and alongside a metal fence towards Burn Brae. The way through the grounds of Burn Brae follows a pebble pathway and is waymarked as far as a ruined cottage (complete with interior bench) beside a kissing-gate.

Through the gate strike across the ensuing field to a hedge gap and then maintain the same direction in the next, towards some farm buildings (**Scholaby** Farm) and a metal gate, beside which there is a stone stile. Now take to the ongoing

In the 1960s, this was just a small farmstead, but, like so many similar places on the island it has since been extensively renovated.

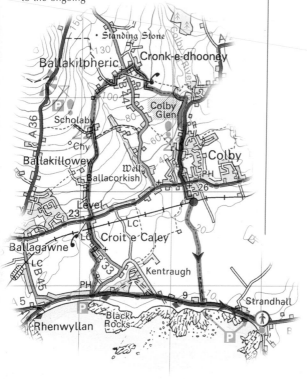

farm access, a long, descending track that eventually reaches the end of a surfaced lane at **Ballacorkish** Farm. Continue down to reach a road junction, turn right and shortly go left at **Level** Garage into **Croit e Caley**.

> Above the access lane descending from Scholaby Farm stands the chimney and ruins of the **Ballacorkish Mine**. This was one of the more successful of the island's mines and produced lead and zinc from three shafts, which reached a maximum depth of 140m (459ft). Work here ceased about 1895, when global competition made the mine unprofitable.

Walk along the road, shortly crossing the line of the steam railway, passing Strawberry Fields and Strawberry Meadows, and continuing as far as a branching road on the right, with a footpath signpost nearby. Walk down to a metal gate, beside which there is a kissing-gate into a field. Bear left along the field edge to a corner hedge gap, and through this follow the left-hand edge of the next pasture to another kissing-gate. Maintain the same direction, now alongside a stream flanked by tall stands of rushes (phragmites).

Eventually the main coast road is reached near the Shore Hotel. Turn left, crossing the road with care, to follow the roadside footpath around the edge of the Bay ny Carrickey to return to the starting point.

WALK 36

Scarlett Point

Start/Finish	Scarlett (SC 258 666)
Distance	5km (3 miles)
Height gain	35m (115ft)
Refreshments	Castletown (via alternative route)
Parking	near Scarlett Point

With sea wind forever tussling your hair, even on the calmest days, this walk is invigorating and refreshing, providing scope for some useful sea- and inland bird watching, or the chance to lie back beside the path and watch aircraft at Ronaldsway come and go. Its brevity leaves time for a full and proper exploration of Castletown, the former capital of the Isle of Man, and a place full of interest. There is, too, considerable geological interest along this section of coastline.

SCARLETT POINT

The name Scarlett Point derives from the Norse word *skarfakluft*, meaning 'cormorant's cleft', a title still appropriate today – the rocks are favoured resting places not only of cormorants, but of shag, little auk, herring and black-backed gulls. Records show that Scarlett Point was one of the Norse 'Day Watch' hills, an early day coastguard lookout post.

The coastline is dominated by Carboniferous limestone laid down between 363 and 325 million years ago and formed from sediments at the bottom of warm, shallow tropical seas at a time when the Isle of Man, like much of Britain, was much farther south than it is today. A distinctive feature of this type of limestone is its layered appearance, clearly visible near the lookout station. The end of limestone deposition throughout the Isle of Man was marked by the explosive eruption of a volcano, which formed the basaltic rocks now exposed between Scarlett and Poyllvaaish. This is especially evident just beyond the lookout station, where the geology distinctly changes from layered Carboniferous limestone to rough-textured basalt deposited by early Tertiary volcanism between 65.5 and 1.8 million years ago. Vents and fissures along which magma flowed to the surface can be seen in the area.

Remain on the seaward side of a high wall. When the wall changes direction near a group of derelict buildings, keep forward on a grassy path, passing the stony remains of a burial mound before pressing on to a ladder/stile spanning a wall.

Cross the next pasture and, in the third, follow the edge of an arable field. Keep going to reach a large earthwork, the remains of a small promontory fort with a ditch. Just beyond it another ladder/stile gives on to a breakwater footpath at the edge of the **Poyllvaaish** Quarry.

> The rocks at Poyllvaaish have seen much volcanic activity and, as a result, have been metamorphosed at least three times. Although a limestone, the black beds of rock became known as **Poyllvaaish Marble**, which found its way into many of the grander homes on the island, into masons' factories to be fashioned in gravestones and even to form the steps of St Paul's Cathedral in London. Alas, the rock weathers poorly, and while the steps of St Paul's had to be replaced, the gravestones simply lost their inscriptions.

After passing the quarry a rough track leads on. Follow it only as far as a signed track on the right, heading across the edge of an arable field. Stay on the track as far as the next signpost, near an old gateway, and here leave the track by turning towards a concrete stile in a field corner. In the ensuing field, go forward along the left-hand field edge alongside a drainage ditch. Over a ladder/stile keep on in the same direction in the next field, passing stands of reeds to reach a step/stile. ▸

This is a good place to look and listen for sedge and grasshopper warbler in early spring.

Over the stile continue in the same direction, then follow the field edge round to a gap and step/stile at an old gateway giving into the adjoining field. Turn into this and go round the edge of the field to a pillbox. There pass through two gates, and turn right to a stone through-stile, and then head up the right-hand edge of the next field to a stile near a former windmill and **Castle Rushen High School**.

Alternative route via Castletown

Over the stile at the rear of the high school, turn left and walk out to a road. Go through a kissing-gate and turn right, walking toward Castletown centre.

CASTLETOWN

Castle Rushen dominates the ancient settlement of Castletown, the hub of Manx politics and power until Douglas assumed that role in the 19th century. The castle, a formidable structure, was home to many Manx kings, and was built largely during the 13th and 14th centuries, although some parts are older.

The town stands at the outflow of the Silverburn River, and many of the town's historic buildings are grouped around the harbour, notably the old grammar school, the oldest intact building on the island. In the days when Castletown was the capital, the island was governed from the House of Keys, now known as the 'Old' House of Keys, and recently restored to its former state so that visitors may see how the island was governed and learn something of its unique political system.

On the edge of town, leave the main road and turn right onto Scarlett Road, passing rows of attractive cottages before finally breaking free of them and pressing on along the edge of Castletown Bay to return to the starting point.

Behind the school turn right along an enclosed footpath ending at another ladder/stile and gate. Go left here and follow the field edge, changing direction twice, to intercept a broad track flanked by low wall. This runs out to meet the Scarlett Point road. ◄ Turn right to return to the starting point.

The alternative route via Castletown rejoins the main route here.

WALK 37
Silverdale Glen

Start/Finish	Silverdale Glen (SC 275 710)
Distance	8km (5 miles)
Height gain	130m (425ft)
Refreshments	Café at start
Parking	At start (limited)

Although one of the highlights of this walk is the opportunity to visit the historic Rushen Abbey, the real beauty lies in pastoral wandering across farmland south of Grenaby followed by exquisite walking in the company of the Silver Burn through the lovely Silverdale Glen. The upper part of the glen is heady with the scent of wild garlic, bright with wild flowers and loud with birdsong. Here the Silver Burn fashions an enchanting course through a lightly wooded dale and the accompanying path cavorts along its flanks, sometimes close by the burn, at others high above it, but never far from its sight. The lower stretch of the glen is more 'managed'. Here, well-trodden footpaths lead beside the burn, past the Monks' Well to the Monks' Bridge and Rushen Abbey itself.

The walk begins from close by the restaurant and children's play area and boating lake on the site of an old watermill, between the upper and lower glens. Turn right from the parking area and a few strides further on bear left into Silverdale Glen: a higher parallel path, used by the

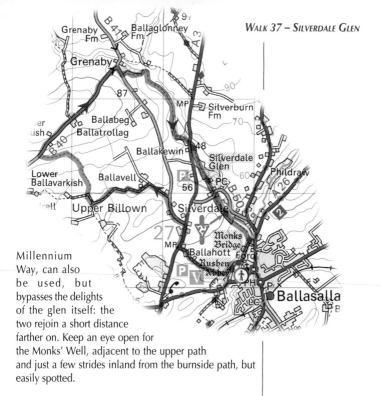

Millennium
Way, can also
be used, but
bypasses the delights
of the glen itself: the
two rejoin a short distance
farther on. Keep an eye open for
the Monks' Well, adjacent to the upper path
and just a few strides inland from the burnside path, but
easily spotted.

Taking its name from the Silver Burn – the *Awin Argid* in Manx – which runs through it, **Silverdale Glen** is rightly one of the delights of the Manx countryside. Near the start an old watermill has been converted to a café and restaurant, with a boating lake and children's play area nearby. One of the features here is a Victorian water-powered carousel, with horses that date from the beginning of the 20th century. This is believed to be the only existing example of this type of roundabout in the world. The lower glen was given to the Manx National Trust in 1964 and contains a small well, the Monks' Well, just aside from the burn.

The glen paths, having joined forces, eventually lead out to a narrow gateway to meet the Millennium Way. Here, turn left: the path wanders on, never far from the sight or sound of the burn, and in due course reaches the lovely double-arched **Monks' Bridge**.

> **Monks' Bridge**, also known as The Crossag – 'little crossing' in Manx – was built in 1350 by the Cistercian monks of Rushen Abbey. The pack-horse bridge allowed the monks to pass over the Silverburn River near Rushen Abbey in Ballasalla so they could travel to their northern farms. It is believed to be the best example of medieval bridge in the British Isles.

From the bridge, continue forward along a surfaced lane. The lane comes out to meet a road adjoining the Abbey Restaurant. On the left is a footbridge and a ford, and beyond that the centre of **Ballasalla**. But the route lies forward, passing the restaurant and soon reaching the entrance to Rushen Abbey and Gardens.

Monk's Bridge, Rushen Abbey

RUSHEN ABBEY

King Olaf I (known as 'Olaf the Dwarf') gave land for the founding of an abbey at Ballasalla in 1134, as a daughter house of Furness in Lancashire (as it then was). A date stone at the side of The Crossag commemorates this date. This marked the beginning of the infiltration of monastic orders into island life. Like Furness, Rushen Abbey was originally of the Savignian (Benedictine) Order but it, too, in time became a Cistercian monastery. The grounds here contain the graves of three Viking kings of Mann who died between 1235 and 1265. The Cistercians were essentially manual workers, accepting neither tithes nor revenue, and proved to be outstanding 'farmers', as Rushen Abbey demonstrated, becoming by far the strongest force on the island, and the controller of all the best farm land: it also took charge of all mining and fishing and, with an abbot who was a baron in his own right, had the power of life and death.

The monks at Rushen Abbey were responsible for the earliest recorded history of the island, the *Chronicon Manniae*, which extended from the laying of the first foundation stone until 1374. Over the subsequent years, however, the abbey became less important, though its abbot and the last six brothers tenaciously held out against Henry VIII's dissolution of the monasteries longer than any other, being forcibly ejected in 1540.

Continue past the abbey to meet the main road. For safety's sake, cross the road with care to a memorial opposite, and turn right, but walk only as far as the next turning on the right (at a poorly sighted left bend). Re-cross with care, ignore the road on the right, and turn instead up a stony track that climbs briefly to a stone stile and kissing-gate at the rear of a couple of houses. Over the stile, go left along a path leading along an enclosed field edge and, later, enclosed between low walls and hedgerows. At a gate with an unusual stile beside it, keep forward along a broad farm track leading to **Ballahott** Farm.

Pass through the farmyard and walk out to meet the Foxdale to Castletown road. Turn right, walking beside the road for about 275m, as far as the next turning on the left (signposted to Grenaby). Walk along the road until, just before Briarfield, you can branch left onto a signposted footpath, in the form of a surfaced lane that leads to **Ballavell** Farm. At the entrance to Ballavell Farm the track swings left, passing Elm Bank, where the road surfacing ends, and then meanders across countryside flanked in spring and early summer by lady's smock, primrose, celandine, bluebell, yellow iris, wood sorrel, bugle and violet. Continue with the track until it forks (SC 262 708) and then bear right. Shortly, when it bends left, leave it by turning right through a metal kissing-gate at a three-way signpost, and walk up the right-hand edge of the ensuing field.

At the top of the field cross two stiles and, in the next field, turn right, following the field edge to the far corner to tackle two more stiles. Cross the end of the next field to another stile giving onto a wooden footbridge and, over this, keep to the right-hand side of the next field to a gate giving onto a road. Now turn right and follow the road for about 1km (½ mile) to a T-junction.

Turn right for less than 100m and then cross a ladder/stile on the left and walk across the end of a field to a signpost at the top of a path descending towards the Silver Burn set in a woodland dell below. There is no need to descend to the burn at this point. Just stay above the valley slope for now, parallel with an old field boundary (waymark on tree); before long the route is fed into an enclosed path at a field edge high above the burn, which it soon descends to reach.

The next stage of the walk, in the shape of a narrow grassy path, follows the course of the Silver Burn. ◄

The burnside path eases along to a ladder/stile. Cross this and bear left to another stile, which gives into a muddy corner among trees from which the path bears right before returning to a course parallel with and above the burn.

The path undulates across slopes dominated by pungent springtime garlic, finally to reach a gate giving into broadleaved woodland. Eventually it comes down to a small clearing with steps down onto a broad track leading, right, out to the Foxdale–Castletown road.

The path is a delight to follow: the route twists and turns, climbs and descends, is muddy and slippery in places, but never loses any of the magical quality that walking of this calibre brings.

Silverdale Glen

Cross with care and go onto the track opposite, re-entering the **Silverdale Glen** and rejoining the Millennium Way. Keep following an obvious path and when you reach the Silverdale Glen Mineral Water Factory cross a small bridge, passing to the right of the boating lake to return to the starting point.

WALK 38

Port Grenaugh, Port Soldrick and
Cass ny Hawin

Start/Finish	Port Grenaugh (SC 316 706)
Distance	6km (3¾ miles)
Height gain	225m (740ft)
Parking	Car park at Port Grenaugh

It isn't long before the thoughts of anyone wandering the coastal cliffs of the island turn to the history of smuggling, a trade in which the islanders were key players. Along this walk we pass Jackdaw Cave, just at the entrance to Port Soldrick, which was a hideaway much favoured by smugglers.

The coastal scenery is outstanding and popular with birds, notably chough, which often gather in flocks, gulls, fulmars...and cormorants, which adopt affected poses on water's edge rocks.

From the road end at **Port Grenaugh**, turn right across a footbridge to follow the Raad ny Foillan along the edge of the pebbly beach to gain a rising path on the other side, climbing onto the headland.

Continue following the coastal path, which occasionally moves into adjacent fields, and back again, and then finds a way to and around **Port Soldrick**. ◀

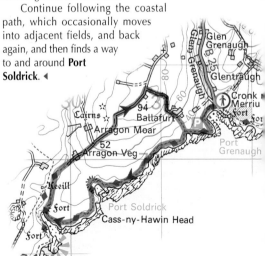

150

Just at the entrance to **Port Soldrick** a fine sea cave appears on the east side of the cove. This is Jackdaw Cave, a genuine smuggler's hideout into which boats would sail, to be loaded via a hole in the roof of the cave.

Port Grenaugh: a delightful place, rarely visited

Gradually the path moves round to meet the narrow and long inlet of **Cass ny Hawin**, where the Santon Burn flows into the sea. Dense stands of gorse fill the air with the heady scent of coconut, cinnamon or nutmeg (according to nasal sensitivities – we all seem to identify different things). Through the gorse, the path steadily works a way upstream.

Confronted with a choice of turning right into a field, or going left down towards the burn, turn left. The path accompanying the burn is a delight to follow, if sometimes a little muddy, and leads to a bridge spanning the burn, where the coastal path goes left. Here, keep forward on a broad grassy track. A short way further on it joins a rutted vehicle track. Turn left along this, which in turn leads out to a surfaced lane.

Turn up the lane, keeping an eye open for a prominent hut circle mound topped with rocks in a field on
the left. Remain on the lane and, about 100m after a derelict cottage on the right, turn right on a road to **Ballafurt**.
Head down past Ballafurt Cottage and then a metal gate
to a ladder/stile giving into a large field. Keep to the left-
hand edge of the field until it becomes possible to switch
sides into an adjacent field, now following the right-hand
edge to rejoin the coastal path at a kissing-gate. Now
simply turn left and retrace your outward route back to
Port Grenaugh.

WALK 39
Port Grenaugh and Santon Head

Start/Finish	Port Grenaugh (SC 316 706)
Distance	6.75km (4¼ miles)
Height gain	225m (740ft)
Parking	Car park at Port Grenaugh

Port Grenaugh is a rarely visited nook tucked away on the south coast of the
island. The walk follows a splendid stretch of the coastal path, but begins by
heading across country before turning for the sea.

At Port Grenaugh, turn through an ornate kissing-gate
onto a narrow path, rising beside a stream, and soon
crossing the stream twice in quick succession as a gravel
path leads up through an attractively cultivated interlude
to another kissing-gate. Through this turn left and follow
a broad track to another gate adjacent to **Arragon House**.
Go forward past the house to a T-junction, and turn right.
    Go through a gate beside a cattle grid and then keep
forward on a broad vehicle track. Go as far as another
ornamental gate (SC 322 708: **Meary Voar**) and cross
a stile beside it. Go forward along a surfaced lane to a

crossroads (SC 329 702), and there turn left onto a surfaced lane (following the course of overhead electricity powerlines). The lane rises to meet a concrete road. Turn left and continue following the road to a crossroads, where the track intercepts the Raad ny Foillan (SC 326 722).

Turn right, climbing gently for a while along a surfaced lane flanked by gorse embankments, vivid with colour in spring and early summer. Continue until the road levels, and then leave it by turning right at a signposted footpath on the right, crossing a stone step/stile to head down a broad vehicle track to a ladder/stile beside a gate. Over this, go forward alongside a gorse hedge on the left, finally rising to a gate in a field corner. Through this turn right for a sudden and stunning view of the coast, especially to the left where the crags of **Pistol Castle** put on a fine display.

The path soon descends through gorse which at some times of year can partially obscure the path, which is narrow and often close to the cliff edge. The gorse can take its toll of bare legs, too, but is interspersed with grassy oases on which it is delightful to sit and watch the birds that frequent the rocks below – cormorants, chough, fulmar, herring gull. Sea thrift grows everywhere, along with squill,

Gorse-lined track to Santon Head

scarlet pimpernel and celandine, while most of the walls display a healthy mantle of mosses.

Now simply enjoy following the ongoing coastal path through all its twists and turns, ups and downs, heading towards the conspicuous inlet of Grenaugh Cove. Just before reaching it, a large mound on the left of the path alerts you to something intriguing. This is **Cronk ny Merriu**, an Iron Age fort, beyond which the path descends via stiles to the road end back in **Port Grenaugh**.

> Occupying a prominent position along the south coast, **Cronk ny Merriu** is a fortified promontory fort with defensive ditch and rampart. The defences were probably Iron Age or from the first few centuries AD. There are also the foundations of a Viking house (10th–11th century) within the fort. It was this period of occupation that gave the cove its name: Port Grenaugh is Norse for 'green creek'.

WALK 40

Derbyhaven, St Michael's Island
and Langness

Start/Finish	Derbyhaven (SC 284 676)
Distance	variable up to 8km (5 miles)
Height gain	Nominal
Refreshments	Derbyhaven
Parking	Derbyhaven

This is a walk with no set route description, but it would be quite unthinkable to produce a book of walks to the Isle of Man without suggesting an exploration of the peninsula of Langness and adjacent St Michael's Island. It is possible to drive to a parking area at SC 284 660 and this will avoid having to walk across a golf course, but there is a good surfaced road across the course, and on a fine, sunny day the whole of this isolated part of the island can consume far more time than the distance involved might suggest. Take a picnic and a pair of binoculars, and perch among the rocks of Langness Point if it's serious chilling out you're in search of; this is the southernmost point of the Isle of Man, excluding the Calf of Man.

Derbyhaven is a neat gathering of houses and cottages built on the neck of land between Castletown Bay and the bay of Derby Haven. A road runs south from the village around the southern edge of **Derby Haven**, passing a golfing hotel, and continues across a causeway – strong winds and a high tide are good times to avoid, if you don't want a drenching here – onto **St Michael's Island**. The island is a small grassy appendage but contains **Derby Fort**, a round fortification, along with the ruins of St Michael's **Chapel**.

Once the island's chief fishing port, **Derbyhaven** was the port of the Derby family, established by the 2nd Earl, Thomas III, in 1507. During the time of the Norsemen, the place was known as *Rognvald's*

Vagir, or Ronald's Way – the name now given to the island's airport – and, like the airport, it saw many landings on the island. The port was the scene, in 1275, of a battle in which John de Vesci, agent of Alexander of Scotland, having failed to negotiate with the Manxmen over the question of Scottish rule of the island, slaughtered over 500 men and brought their revolt to an end.

The rocks of Castletown Bay are a good place to look for birdlife, while, further out, you may spot the occasional seal or harbour porpoise.

Go back towards Derbyhaven, but before reaching the first houses, take a road on the left which curves sharply southwards and heads across the golf course. ◄

Go as far as the parking area, and just beyond it, leave the surfaced road, to bear right along the edge of Castletown Bay out to **Langness Point**: a clear grassy path shows the way.

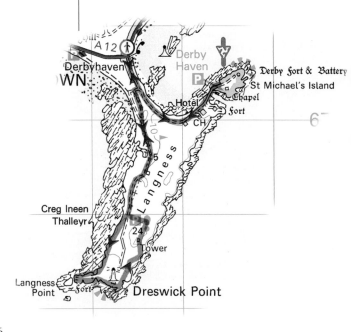

The 'Herring Tower'

The long peninsula of **Langness** has a splendid coastline of rocks and caves, and has at its extreme point a reef called the Skerranes, where many a ship has come to grief. The prominent cylindrical tower was built in 1816 as a landmark for shipping before the building of the lighthouse, and is known locally as the Herring Tower.

From the southern end of Langness, head back towards **Dreswick Point** and the lighthouse, the last lighthouse on the island to be automated. Keep to the path that passes around the lighthouse perimeter, and continue up

Coastline, Langness

the eastern coastline, passing the Round Tower, shortly after which, at a Raad ny Foillan signpost, branch left to return to the parking area passed earlier, and there join the road back out across the golf course. Alternatively, go past the sign and bear right to the coastal rocks a short distance farther on to reach a carved rock, a memorial for the schooner 'Provider', shipwrecked here in 1853 while on a voyage carrying salt from Liverpool to Glasgow.

Numerous grassy trails lead from this area inland to intercept the peninsula road, although the easiest is to retrace your steps to the Raad ny Foillan signpost.

APPENDIX A

Route summary table

No	Title		Distance	Height gain	Page
1	Ayres, Point of Ayre and Bride	Ayres Visitor Centre (NX 435 038)	12km (7½ miles)	80m (262ft)	26
2	Sulby and the Millennium Way	Sulby Claddagh (SC 386 940)	10km (6¼ miles)	358m (1175ft)	29
3	Slieu Curn and Slieu Dhoo	Ballaugh (SC 348 935)	17.3km (10¾ miles)	445m (1460ft)	32
4	Orrisdale and Glen Trunk	Orrisdale (SC 327 929)	4.4km (2¾ miles)	55m (180ft)	36
5	Kirk Michael and Slieau Freoaghane	Kirk Michael (SC 319 909)	14.5km (9 miles)	533m (1750ft)	39
6	Slieau Freoaghane and Sartfell	Sartfell Plantation (SC 342 866)	5.3km (3½ miles)	215m (705ft)	42
7	Sulby Reservoir	Sulby Reservoir car park (SC 374 890)	4.25km (2½ miles)	257m (343ft)	44
8	Upper Sulby Glen	Sulby Reservoir car park (SC 374 890)	12km (7½ miles)	443m (1453ft)	46
9	A taste of the Millennium Way	Bungalow (SC 396 868)	11km (7 miles)	210m 690ft)	48
10	Maughold Brooghs and Port Mooar	Maughold (SC 490 917)	7.3km (4½ miles)	290m (950ft)	52
11	Cornaa and Ballaglass Glen	Cornaa (SC 466 899)	7km (4¼ miles)	215m (705ft)	56
12	Dhoon Glen	A2 road bend at Dhoon (SC 452 863)	2.25km (1½ miles)	190m (625ft)	59
13	Clagh Ouyr and North Barrule	Black Hut (SC 406 885)	9.5km (6 miles)	505m (1657ft)	62
14	Snaefell from the Bungalow	Bungalow (SC 396 868)	6.8km (4½ miles)	405m (1329ft)	64

159

No	Title		Distance	Height gain	Page
28	South Barrule Forest Walk and Corlea Plantation	South Barrule Plantation (SC 275 767)	8.5km (5¼ miles)	315m (1033ft)	107
29	Lhiattee ny Beinnee and Fleshwick Bay	The Sloc road bend (SC 217 733)	8.4km (5¼ miles)	457m (1500ft)	111
30	Bradda Head and Bradda Hill	Bradda Glen car park (SC 192 697)	5.5km (3½ miles)	280m (920ft)	113
31	Port Erin to Peel	Port Erin railway station (SC 197 689)	22.7km (14 miles)	1250m (4100ft)	117
32	Mull Hill, Spanish Head and The Chasms	Port Erin (SC 195 690)	8.5km (5¼ miles)	303m (994ft)	124
33	Mull Hill and Cregneash	Cregneash village car park (SC 191 675)	2.5km (1½ miles)	70m (230ft)	129
34	Port St Mary, The Sound and Port Erin	Port St Mary (SC 211 672)	10.5km (6½ miles)	492m 1614ft)	132
35	Colby Glen, Ballakilpheric and Bay ny Carrickey	Bay ny Carrickey (SC 239 686)	8.7km (5½ miles)	145m (475ft)	137
36	Scarlett Point	Scarlett (SC 258 666)	5km (3 miles)	35m (115ft)	141
37	Silverdale Glen	Silverdale Glen (SC 275 710)	8km (5 miles)	130m (425ft)	144
38	Port Grenaugh, Port Soldrick and Cass ny Hawin	Port Grenaugh (SC 316 706)	6km (3¾ miles)	225m (740ft)	150
39	Port Grenaugh and Santon Head	Port Grenaugh (SC 316 706)	6.75km (4¼ miles)	225m (740ft)	152
40	Derbyhaven, St Michael's Island and Langness	Derbyhaven (SC 284 676)	Variable up to 8km (5 miles)	Nominal	155

APPENDIX B
Longer waymarked walks

Established in 1979, the **Millennium Way** was the first long-distance footpath created on the island, and was timed to celebrate the Millennium Year of the Manx parliament, Tynwald. The path links Ramsey to Castletown, following as closely as possible the route of Manx kings through the centre of the island (Ramsey was a safe anchorage, much favoured by the Norse kings: Castle Rushen in Castletown was the royal residence). The route is an early highway with a long and ancient history. Once known as the Royal Way, it is recorded in the 13th-century *Chronicles of the Kings of Mann and the Isles*.

The Way starts from Castle Rushen in Castletown and passes through Ballasalla, Silverdale Glen, Crosby and Baldwin before reaching Ramsey, a distance of 45km (28 miles), well within the day capabilities of experienced long distance walkers, but also easily adapted to a two- or three-day itinerary using public transport at the end of each day. The final stage from Baldwin is across open moorland, requiring walkers to be fully equipped for all eventualities.

Raad ny Foillan ('The Road of the Gull') runs around the coast of the island and embraces some truly spectacular scenery on the way. It is 153km (95 miles) of superb walking, not too demanding, and do-able comfortably in eight days. The Raad ny Foillan was opened in 1986 to mark the island's Heritage Year, but the idea of a coastal footpath was mooted much earlier, by Sir Ambrose Dundas Flux Dundas, a former governor of the island and enthusiastic rambler.

The coastline of the island is rightly regarded as a national treasure by the Manx, so you'll encounter little that detracts from its natural beauty. The route follows the coastline as much as possible, from the shingle beaches at the northern end of the island to 180m (591ft) high hills and cliffs above The Sloc.

Bayr ny Skeddan ('The Herring Road') is based on a route taken by the Manx fishermen as they journeyed between Castletown and Peel. Weighing in at a mere 23km (14¼ miles), this is a walk that most fit walkers can complete in a day. Initially following the Millennium Way, the Bayr ny Skeddan heads north after Silverdale Glen and strikes across the moorland divide near the Round Table and South Barrule. It then heads for Glen Maye, where it meets up with the Raad ny Foillan for the final leg into Peel.

The **Heritage Trail** runs for a modest 18km (11 miles) from the outskirts of Douglas, using the route of the defunct Isle of Man Railway Company's lines to Peel. The first half mile or so has now been built over, and it is only at Quarterbridge that the original route is joined. On its journey to Peel, the trail passes through delightful countryside and enjoys a succession of woodland and floral oases. Although the walk can be completed easily enough in a day, there are plenty of opportunities to break out to the A1 main road and take a bus back to your starting point, notably at Glen Vine, Crosby and St John's.

The **Ramsey Line** is a walk of 29km (18 miles) from Ramsey to St John's, following the course of the Manx Northern Railway opened in 1879.

APPENDIX C
Useful contacts

Isle of Man tourism
The Welcome Centre
Sea Terminal
Douglas
IM1 2RG
Open Monday to Saturday all year, Easter Sunday,
and Sundays from April to the last Sunday in September.
Tel 01624 686766;
www.visitisleofman.com

In addition the Isle of Man government website –
www.gov.im – has a comprehensive index of services,
facilities and attractions across the island.

Tourist information offices

Open all year
Airport
Tel 01624 821600

Castletown Civic Centre
Farrants Way
Castletown
IM9 1NR
Open Monday to Saturday
Tel 01624 825005

Port Erin
12 Bridson Street
Port Erin
IM9 6AN
Open Monday to Friday
Tel 01624 832298 or 835858

Onchan Library
Willow House
Main Road
Onchan
IM3 1AJ
Open Monday to Saturday
Tel 01624 621228

Port St Mary
Town Hall
Promenade
Port St Mary
IM9 5DA
Open Monday to Friday
Tel 01624 832101

Peel
Town Hall
Derby Road
Peel
IM9 1RG
Open Monday to Friday
Tel 01624 842341

Ramsey Library
West Street
Ramsey
IM8 1AE
Open Monday to Saturday
Tel 01624 817025

Summer only
Ballasalla
Tel 01624 822531

Other information sources
Laxey Heritage Trust
Old Fire House
Mines Road
Laxey
IM4 7NJ
Open Easter to September
Tel 01624 862007

Manx National Heritage
Manx Museum
Kingswood Grove
Douglas
IM1 3LY
Tel 01624 648000
www.manxnationalheritage.im

Manx Wildlife Trust
7–8 Market Place
Peel
IM5 1AB
Tel 01624 844432
www.manxwt.org.uk

The Manx Wildlife Trust is the island's leading nature conservation charity, tasked with informing and educating about the importance of Manx wildlife and natural habitats. The Trust is responsible for the maintenance of 22 nature reserves across the island, eight of which are open to the public. The Trust's marine team collects data on basking sharks and marine mammals around the island, logging sightings and promoting the importance of protecting the animals and their environment. This work includes the study of the largest grey seal breeding colony in Manx waters, at the Calf of Man.

The Trust also promotes the protection of flora, from wild flowers to ancient woodlands, to ensure species continue to thrive throughout the island.

APPENDIX D
Further reading

The Ancient and Historic Monuments (Manx National Heritage, 4th edition, 1973)

Clucas, SD *The Thousla Cross* (Rushen Parish Commissioners, 1982)

Cubbon, AM *The Art of the Manx Crosses* (Manx National Heritage, 3rd edition, 1983)

Evans, A *Isle of Man Coastal Path* (Cicerone Press, 1991)

Freeman, TW et al *Lancashire, Cheshire and the Isle of Man* (Thomas Nelson, 1966)

Kneale, Trevor *The Isle of Man* (Pevensey Island Guide, 2001)

Prehistoric Sites in the Isle of Man (Manx National Heritage, 4th impression, 1986)

Rimington, John *Features and History of the Meayll Peninsula* (Rushen Parish Commissioners, 2000)

The Royal Chapel of St John the Baptist: A Short History and Guide to 'The Tynwald Church'

Salter, M *Castles and Old Churches of the Isle of Man* (Folly Publications, 1997)

Stenning, EH *Portrait of the Isle of Man* (Robert Hale, 1958, 1965, 1975 and 1978)

Young, GVC *A Brief History of the Isle of Man* (Mansk-Svenska Publishing, Peel, 2nd edition, 1999)

APPENDIX E

Glossary of Manx terms and place names

Most of the place names found on the Isle of Man have Gaelic origins and serve as a reminder that the Manx Gaelic language was once widely spoken here. Other names are of Norse origin, especially those that refer to coastal features. Places like Foxdale have been Anglicised, in this case from *fors dala*, 'waterfall dale'. Elsewhere, you'll find names that are distinctly English, and a few that distinctly are not.

Manx Gaelic	English
a	river (as in Laxa, Cornaa, Rumsa, Crogga)
ard	height
ayre	gravel beach
balla	farm, place (of)
beg, veg	little
br>ogh	bank, brow
byr, by	homestead (as in Crosby)
cashtal	castle
claddagh	river meadow
creg, creggan	rock
croit	croft
cronk	hill
curragh	marsh, bogland
fell	mountain (as in Sartfell)
garroo	rough

Manx Gaelic	English
glion	glen
gob	point, promontory
howe	headland
keeill	chapel
kerroo	quarterland
knock	hillock
lag, laggan	hollow
logh	lake
mooar, vooar	great, big
pooyl	pool
purt, phurt	port, harbour
reeast	moorland
sallagh	willow
slieau	mountain
spooyt	waterfall
stakkr	sea stack
vik	creek

SOME MANX PLACE NAMES	
Agneash (Scand)	*eggjornes* (edge ness); *ness* (nose/promontory)
Arragon (Old Irish)	O'Rogan's river-mouth
Baldwin (Scand)	*bol* (homestead); *dalr* (dale)
Baldromma (Manx)	*balla* (farm/place of); *drommey* (ridge)
Ballacallin (Manx)	*balla* (farm/place of); *callin* – Macallyn
Ballacreggan (Manx)	*balla* (farm/place of); *creggan* (stones)
Ballachurry (Manx)	*balla* (farm/place of); *churry/charry* (mire/dung)
Ballacuberagh (Manx)	*balla* (farm/place of); Coobragh – Cuthbert
Ballacurnkeil (Manx)	*balla* (farm/place of); *curn* (Curry's); *keil* (of the church)
Ballfurt (Manx)	*balla* (farm/place of); *phurt* (port/harbour)
Ballaglass (Manx)	*balla* (farm/place of); *glass* (green – green farm)
Ballagrawe (Manx)	*balla* (farm/place of); *ny* (of the); *gro* (acorns)
Ballakilley (Manx)	*balla* (farm/place of); *keeil* (church)
Ballakilpheric (Manx)	*balla* (farm/place of); *keeil* (church); Pheric (Patrick)
Ballameanagh (Manx)	*balla* (farm/place of); *meanagh* (middle)
Ballaragh (Manx)	*balla* (farm/place of); *arraght* (ghost)
Ballasalla (Manx)	*balla* (farm/place of); *sallagh* (sallies: reeds/rushes)
Ballaugh/Ballalough (Manx)	*balley ny loughy* (place of the lake/lough)
Ballavarane (Manx)	*balla* (farm/place of); Verane (obsolete Irish name)
Ballavell (Manx)	*balla* (farm/place of); *vell* (corruption of Bell – Bell's farm)
Ballayolgane (Manx)	balley (farm/place of); *yolgane* (Golgane's – old Irish surname)
Balleira (Manx)	*balla* (farm/place of); *leira* (muddy stream)
Bay ny Carricky (Manx)	*bay ny* (bay of); *carricky* (stones)
Bayr Glass (Manx)	*bayr* (road); *glass* (green – green road)
Block Eary (Scand)	*block* (black); *eary* (sheiling)
Bradda (Norse)	*bratthaugr* (steep headland)
Carn Vael (Manx)	*carn* (cairn); Vael (Michael – Michael's cairn)

SOME MANX PLACE NAMES	
Carrick(ey) (Manx)	a sea-rock (Carrick Rock – a sea-rock rock!)
Cashtel Mooar (Manx)	*cashtel* (castle); *mooar/vooar* (big)
Cass ny Hawin (Manx)	*cass* (fort); *ny* (of the), *hawin* (river)
Clagh Ouyr (Manx)	*clagh* (stone); *ouyr* (dunn coloured – brown stone)
Close ny Chollagh (Manx)	*close* (enclosure); *ny* (of the); *chollagh* (stallions)
Colby (Scand)	*col* (Kolli's); *byr* (farm)
Cooildarry (Manx)	*cooil* (hidden place); *darrag* (bog oaks)
Corlea (Manx)	*cor* (hill); *lleagh* (grey)
Cregneash (Manx)	*creg* (rock); *ny* (of); *eash* (ages)
Cregneash (Scand)	*krakurness* (promontory of the crows)
Cronkedooney (Manx)	*cronk* (hill); *e* (of the); Dooney (The Lord's Day – Sunday)
Cronk Keeil Abbon (Manx)	*cronk* (hill); *keeil* (church); Abbon (saint's name)
Cronk Koir (Manx)	*cronk* (hill); *koir* (storage chest – sometimes 'kist')
Cronk Moar (Manx)	*cronk* (hill); *moar/mooar* (big)
Cronk ny Arrey Laa (Manx)	*cronk* (hill); *ny* (of the); *arrey-laa* (day-watch; *laa* – day)
Cronk ny Irree Laa (Manx)	*cronk* (hill); *ny* (of the); *irree-laa* (day-break)
Cronk ny Merriu (Manx)	*cronk* (hill); *ny* (of the); *marroo* (dead)
Cronk Shamerk (Manx/Scand)	*cronk* (hill); *shamerk* – *skammhyggr* (short ridge)
Cronk Sumark (Manx)	*cronk* (hill); *sumark* (primrose)
Cronk Urleigh (Manx)	*cronk* (hill); *urleigh* (slaughter (now 'eagle'), by default from the damage caused to the sheep flocks by 'eagles' (though none ever recorded on the island)
Crosby (Scand)	*kros* (cross); *byr* (farm)
Dalby (Scand)	*dal-byr* (dale-farm)
Dreswick (Scand)	*drangsvik* (rock creek)
Eary Cushlin (Manx)	*eary* (sheiling); *cushlin* (Cosnahan's – old surname)
Eyreton (Modern)	Eyre's town – after the owner of the land in 1867
Fleshwick (Scand)	*flesvik* (green creek – pronounced 'fleshik')
Foxdale (Scand)	*fors* (waterfall); dalr (dale)

SOME MANX PLACE NAMES	
Glen Chass (Manx)	*glen* (valley); *shast* (sedges/reeds)
Glen Dhoo (Manx)	*glen* (valley); *dhoo* (black)
Glen Needle (Manx)	*glen* (valley); corruption of MacNeeven
Glen Trunk (Eng)	No known reason; possibly from flotsam on the beach
Glen Wyllin (Manx)	*glen* (valley); *mwyllin* (mill)
Grenaby (Scand)	*grean* (green); *byr* (farm)
Groudle (Scand)	*krappdalr; craudall* (narrow glen)
Howe (Scand)	*howe* (mound)
Keeil ny Traie (Manx)	*keeil* (church); *ny* (of the); *traie* (shore)
Kerrodhoo (Manx)	*kerroo* (quarterland); *dhoo* (black – peaty ground)
Killabrega (Manx)	*keeil* (church); *brega* (Irish saint – Breaga's church)
Langness (Scand)	long promontory (long nose)
Lhiattee ny Bainnee (Manx)	*lhiattee* (the side); *ny* (of); *bainnee* (summit/peak)
Meayll (Mull) (Manx)	*meayll* (bald)
Mount Karrin (Eng/Manx)	*carrin* (cairn – mount of the cairn)
Niarbyl (Manx)	*ny* (the); *arbyl* (tail – of the rocks)
Perwick (Scand)	*purtvik* (harbour creek)
Port Grenaugh (Scand)	*graenvik* (green creek)
Pooyl Vaaish (Manx)	*pooyl/poyll* (pool/bay); *vaaish* (death)
Port Mooar (Manx)	Phurt Mooar (Big Port)
Port Soldrick/Soderick (Scand)	*solvik* (sunny creek)
Port e Vullen (Manx)	Phurt e Vullen (Port of the Mill)
Rushen (Old Eng)	*rushen* (rushes)
Rhyne (Manx)	*rheynn* (ridge)
Sartfell (Scand)	*sart* (dark/black); *fell* (mountain)
Scarlett (Scand)	*skafakleft* (cormorant's cleft)
Scholaby (Scand)	Skolla's *byr* (farm)
Skerranes (Manx)	*skerraneyen* (little sea-rocks)
Slieu Curn (Manx/Irish)	*slieu* (mountain); *curn* (Curryn – Curryn's mountain)

SOME MANX PLACE NAMES	
Slieu Dhoo (Manx)	*slieu* (mountain); dhoo (black)
Slieu Freoaghane (Manx)	*slieu* (mountain); *Freoaghane* (bilberry/blaeberry)
Slieu Ruy (Manx)	*slieu* (mountain); ruy (red)
Slieu Whallian (Old Irish)	*sliabh* (mountain); *ailin* (Aylen – old surname)
Snaefell (Scand)	*snae* (snow); *fell* (mountain)
Spooyt Vane (Manx)	*spooyt* (spout/waterfall); *vane*/bane (white)
Struan ny Fasnee (Manx)	*strooan* (stream); *ny* (of); *fasnee* (winnowing)
Surby (Scand)	*saur* (moorland); *byr* (farm)
Tholt y Will (Manx)	*tolta* (hill); *ny* (of the); *woaillee* (cattle-fold)
Trollaby (Scand)	*trolla* (Trolli's); *byr* (farm)

LISTING OF CICERONE GUIDES

Scrambles in the Lake District
North & South
Short Walks in Lakeland
1 South Lakeland
2 North Lakeland
3 West Lakeland
The Cumbria Coastal Way
The Cumbria Way
Tour of the Lake District

DERBYSHIRE, PEAK DISTRICT AND MIDLANDS
High Peak Walks
Scrambles in the Dark Peak
The Star Family Walks
Walking in Derbyshire
White Peak Walks
The Northern Dales
The Southern Dales

SOUTHERN ENGLAND
Suffolk Coast & Heaths Walks
The Cotswold Way
The Great Stones Way
The North Downs Way
The Peddars Way and Norfolk
Coast Path
The Ridgeway National Trail
The South Downs Way
The South West Coast Path
The Thames Path
The Two Moors Way
Walking in Essex
Walking in Kent
Walking in Norfolk
Walking in Sussex
Walking in the Chilterns
Walking in the Cotswolds
Walking in the Isles of Scilly
Walking in the New Forest
Walking in the Thames Valley
Walking on Dartmoor
Walking on Guernsey
Walking on Jersey
Walking on the Isle of Wight
Walks in the South Downs
National Park

WALES AND WELSH BORDERS
Glyndwr's Way
Great Mountain Days
in Snowdonia
Hillwalking in Snowdonia
Hillwalking in Wales: 1&2
Offa's Dyke Path
Ridges of Snowdonia

Scrambles in Snowdonia
The Ascent of Snowdon
The Ceredigion and Snowdonia
Coast Paths
Lleyn Peninsula Coastal Path
Pembrokeshire Coastal Path
The Severn Way
The Shropshire Hills
The Wye Valley Walk
Walking in Pembrokeshire
Walking in the Forest of Dean
Walking in the South Wales Valleys
Walking in the Wye Valley
Walking on Gower
Walking on the Brecon Beacons
Welsh Winter Climbs

INTERNATIONAL CHALLENGES, COLLECTIONS AND ACTIVITIES
Canyoning
Canyoning in the Alps
Europe's High Points
The Via Francigena: 1&2

EUROPEAN CYCLING
Cycle Touring in France
Cycle Touring in Ireland
Cycle Touring in Spain
Cycle Touring in Switzerland
Cycling in the French Alps
Cycling the Canal du Midi
Cycling the River Loire
The Danube Cycleway Vol 1
The Grand Traverse of the
Massif Central
The Moselle Cycle Route
The Rhine Cycle Route
The Way of St James

AFRICA
Climbing in the Moroccan
Anti-Atlas
Kilimanjaro
Mountaineering in the Moroccan
High Atlas
The High Atlas
Trekking in the Atlas Mountains
Walking in the Drakensberg

ALPS – CROSS-BORDER ROUTES
100 Hut Walks in the Alps
Across the Eastern Alps: E5
Alpine Points of View
Alpine Ski Mountaineering
1 Western Alps
2 Central and Eastern Alps

Chamonix to Zermatt
Snowshoeing
Tour of Mont Blanc
Tour of the Matterhorn
Trekking in the Alps
Trekking in the Silvretta and
Rätikon Alps
Walking in the Alps
Walks and Treks in the
Maritime Alps

PYRENEES AND FRANCE/SPAIN CROSS-BORDER ROUTES
Rock Climbs in the Pyrenees
The GR10 Trail
The GR11 Trail – La Senda
The Mountains of Andorra
The Pyrenean Haute Route
The Pyrenees
The Way of St James:
France & Spain
Walks and Climbs in the Pyrenees

AUSTRIA
The Adlerweg
Trekking in Austria's Hohe Tauern
Trekking in the Stubai Alps
Trekking in the Zillertal Alps
Walking in Austria

BELGIUM AND LUXEMBOURG
Walking in the Ardennes

EASTERN EUROPE
The High Tatras
The Mountains of Romania
Walking in Bulgaria's
National Parks
Walking in Hungary

FRANCE
Chamonix Mountain Adventures
Ecrins National Park
Mont Blanc Walks
Mountain Adventures in
the Maurienne
The Cathar Way
The GR20 Corsica
The GR5 Trail
The Robert Louis Stevenson Trail
Tour of the Oisans: The GR54
Tour of the Queyras
Tour of the Vanoise
Trekking in the Vosges and Jura
Vanoise Ski Touring
Via Ferratas of the French Alps

For full information on all our
guides, books and eBooks,
visit our website:
www.cicerone.co.uk.

Walking – Trekking – Mountaineering – Climbing – Cycling

Over 40 years, Cicerone have built up an outstanding collection of over 300 guides, inspiring all sorts of amazing adventures.

Every guide comes from extensive exploration and research by our expert authors, all with a passion for their subjects. They are frequently praised, endorsed and used by clubs, instructors and outdoor organisations.

All our titles can now be bought as **e-books**, **ePubs** and **Kindle** files and we also have an online magazine – **Cicerone Extra** – with features to help cyclists, climbers, walkers and trekkers choose their next adventure, at home or abroad.

Our website shows any **new information** we've had in since a book was published. Please do let us know if you find anything has changed, so that we can publish the latest details. On our **website** you'll also find great ideas and lots of detailed information about what's inside every guide and you can buy **individual routes** from many of them online.

It's easy to keep in touch with what's going on at Cicerone by getting our monthly **free e-newsletter**, which is full of offers, competitions, up-to-date information and topical articles. You can subscribe on our home page and also follow us on **Facebook** and **Twitter** or dip into our **blog**.

Cicerone – the very best guides for exploring the world.

CICERONE

2 Police Square Milnthorpe Cumbria LA7 7PY
Tel: 015395 62069 info@cicerone.co.uk
www.cicerone.co.uk and **www.cicerone-extra.com**